Effective PR

Angela Murray

For UK order enquiries: please contact Bookpoint Ltd,
130 Milton Park, Abingdon, Oxon OX14 4SB.
Telephone: +44 (0) 1235 827720. Fax: +44 (0) 1235 400454.
Lines are open 09.00–17.00, Monday to Saturday, with a 24-hour
message answering service. Details about our titles and how to
order are available at www.teachyourself.com

Long renowned as the authoritative source for self-guided
learning – with more than 50 million copies sold worldwide –
the **Teach Yourself** series includes over 500 titles in the fields of
languages, crafts, hobbies, business, computing and education.

British Library Cataloguing in Publication Data: a catalogue record
for this title is available from the British Library.

This edition published 2010.

Previously published as *Teach Yourself PR*

The **Teach Yourself** name is a registered trade mark of
Hodder Headline.

Typeset by MPS Limited, a Macmillan Company.

Printed in Great Britain for Hodder Education, an Hachette UK
Company, 338 Euston Road, London NW1 3BH, by CPI Cox &
Wyman, Reading, Berkshire RG1 8EX.

The publisher has used its best endeavours to ensure that the URLs
for external websites referred to in this book are correct and active
at the time of going to press. However, the publisher and the author
have no responsibility for the websites and can make no guarantee
that a site will remain live or that the content will remain relevant,
decent or appropriate.

Hachette UK's policy is to use papers that are natural, renewable
and recyclable products and made from wood grown in sustainable
forests. The logging and manufacturing processes are expected to
conform to the environmental regulations of the country of origin.

Impression number   10 9 8 7 6 5 4 3 2 1

Year   2014 2013 2012 2011 2010

Contents

Meet the author

I have worked in PR for over 20 years – initially with a publishing house, then with a regional, awarding-winning consultancy (where I was a senior consultant) and finally – for the past 15 years – as a freelance working both on my own and as an associate for larger agencies. As a result, not only have I experienced almost every different type of PR activity, but I have also worked with an incredibly wide range of organizations – from the multinational to the one-man-band and everything in between – and seen how PR can boost reputation, sales, morale and much more.

Many organizations already undertake 'typical' PR activities, but without a PR campaign in mind, or without the strategic input or PR experience required to make these activities really effective. Often, PR is considered a glamorous, possibly mysterious profession, irrelevant to the day-to-day operations of many organizations. In fact, PR is based on a set of core skills (which, admittedly, not everyone has) and tried and trusted techniques relevant to everyone. Once you understand how to deploy these skills, then you can unlock PR's real potential, and this book will help you do this.

Angela Murray

Acknowledgements

I would like to thank the following for their invaluable assistance: Richard Hubbard, former journalist and now Global Group Head of Marketing, ISG PLC, for advice on dealing with the media (Chapter 3), and on the use of websites in PR campaigns (Chapters 3 and 4); Chris Lowe, formerly head of Public Affairs for PricewaterhouseCoopers for the information on Government Affairs and Lobbying, Chapter 9 (first edition), and Jonathan Bracken MCIPR, Partner and Head of Public Policy, Bircham Dyson Bell LLP, for his updates and revisions to the same section; and Neil Mainland MCIPR, Broadgate Mainland, for information on Financial PR, also Chapter 9 (first and second editions), and Caroline Cecil, director of financial and corporate PR consultancy Caroline Cecil Associates, and Chair of the CIPR Corporate and Financial Group, for advice on the same section. I also thank HarperCollins Publishers for permission to use the dictionary definition given on page 2.

Finally, I would also like to give special thanks to my family, especially to my daughters Anna and Sarah and to my husband Gerard.

Only got a minute?

Every organization communicates something to someone – even if they do nothing. A Public Relations (PR) strategy, or campaign, aims to improve these communications by identifying who to communicate with (audiences), what to say to them (messages) and how to say it (appropriate activities).

Audiences can be wide-ranging (including customers, supporters, staff, advisers, even the local community), and PR campaign focus can vary tremendously – from one small aspect of your organization (a specific service, for example), to everything you do (including 'corporate PR', used to communicate brand values or corporate ethos). PR works equally well for products as for services, and is also highly effective when used to inform or educate. It is also relevant to all types of organization, including commercial, public sector and not-for-profit.

PR is often associated primarily with 'media liaison' – communicating with journalists – and although this is one aspect of a PR campaign it is often not the only one, sometimes not even the most important. A wide range of other communication tools (such as newsletters or seminars) is also used, as well as corporate hospitality and sponsorship. Internal PR – directed at staff – can also be important, as can crisis management and specialist PR (focusing on finance, or on government lobbying – 'Government Affairs'). Campaign success is determined by how well your messages reach each audience identified, measured in a number of ways, from media coverage to direct feedback.

PR is a strategic management tool, and although activities can be implemented by junior members of staff, management input is essential to maintain that all important momentum. Many organizations employ in-house PR staff, and PR consultancies are frequently used to provide both strategic ideas and administrative support, with the result that PR has become a growing – and popular – career option.

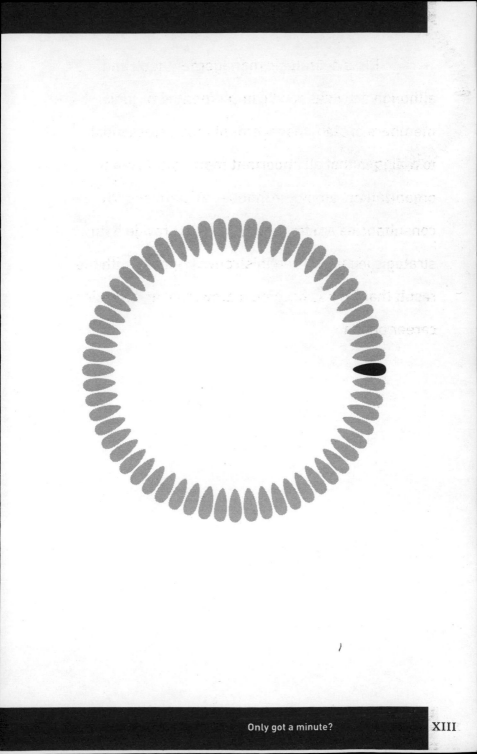

1

Introduction

In this chapter you will learn:
- *what PR is all about*
- *about the benefits PR can deliver*
- *about different types of PR campaign*

Everyone 'does' PR it seems – but what exactly do they do?

This book is written for anyone who (a) knows they should be using PR as part of their marketing strategy but (b) is not sure exactly what it is or (c) how they should evaluate its worth. You probably run, or are part of, a marketing team within a small- or medium-sized organization, commercial or not-for-profit, or are responsible for publicity within a public body, interest group, charity or local community group. Or you may be on the management team, or run your own company – but whatever your role you suspect that you should be using PR more proactively. Perhaps you are already 'doing' PR without really trying – you're receiving press coverage for example – and you know you could be making more of the opportunities on offer. Or perhaps your competitors, or other organizations or individuals just like yourself, are starting to generate the sort of attention which you know you are equally worthy of.

This book will help unravel the mysteries of PR and help you understand what it's all about, what techniques will suit your organization best, and show you how to assess the performance of your PR campaign.

But let's start at the beginning.

What is PR?

Books such as this often begin by quoting a dictionary definition –
and as PR is a term which often proves easy to say, yet hard to
explain, it's as good a way of starting as any. So, what does
Collins English Dictionary say?:

> **public relations** n 1.a the practice of creating, promoting
> or maintaining goodwill and a favourable image among the
> public towards an institution, public body, etc.

As this book unfolds you will see that concepts such as 'goodwill'
and 'public' are key terms which can be defined in many different
ways, but they are nevertheless fundamental to an understanding of
what PR actually is. In a nutshell, PR can be used to the benefit of
almost every aspect of your organization. It can systemize, develop
and improve every conceivable way in which you communicate
with those 'publics' most important to you – whether they are
customers, clients, investors, suppliers, staff or any other interested
groups, including the community in which you are based. Some
organizations employ sizeable teams of both in-house and external
PR professionals to run their campaigns 24 hours a day, seven
days a week – but as this book will demonstrate, in most cases
this simply isn't necessary. It may be that you only have to dip
into your PR file once or twice a year, when you've got something
important to promote, or that you can set up a few PR activities
which will then run themselves happily, needing only regular, low-
key input. Once you've worked your way through this book, it will
be clear as to what is needed in order to make PR work for you.

Let's start by answering a few fundamental questions, in order to
help you understand the reasoning behind PR, and to help you
to start planning your own campaign.

Insight
Use PR to strategically improve every form of communication
used by your organization – the result will be a better

and more supportive relationship between you and your stakeholders, from customers to staff, investors to the local community, and many more besides.

Why practise public relations?

It's rather ironic that PR – the art of promoting a favourable impression – has itself gained quite a poor reputation: it's expensive, it's superficial, it tries to fool a gullible public and it yields results which are impossible to evaluate. Yet almost every major organization, and an increasing number of SMEs (small- or medium-sized enterprises), commit a significant budget to PR year after year – why do they do this?

THE BENEFITS OF GOOD PR

PR can deliver an enormous range of benefits, and it's important to be aware, at a global level, of what can be achieved in order to enable you to plan a strategy that meets the needs of your organization:

Effective, consistent, sustained communication
PR is the art of communication – whether via an appropriate vehicle or 'medium' (such as the media, a website or literature such as a corporate brochure), or face to face at an exhibition, seminar or other event. A PR strategy will ensure that you are exploiting all possible channels of communication as efficiently as possible – that you are making the most of available opportunities; that you are making sure your messages are clear and relevant; and that your communications are consistent across the board. This will not only ensure that the right people know about your organization, but that the image you present is consistent and coherent, improving recognition and credibility. PR is driven by a full appreciation of the ways in which an audience gains information, using this knowledge as the main inspiration for planning campaign activities.

A versatile marketing tool

PR is both versatile and creative, and encourages the use of a wide range of methods in order to get a message across to a target audience, and to get it across in the most efficient way possible.

Maintaining ongoing interest in (and a better understanding of) your organization

PR aims to encourage sustained interest in your organization. By supplying your target audiences with regular information delivered in a variety of ways you can maintain awareness even when you have little new information to promote. This can prove particularly valuable if you are dependent upon high-value, but infrequent, sales or contracts. If the window of opportunity is so small, then you must ensure that your market exposure is continuous so that your name will be recognized when the time to make a decision has arrived.

PR can also be used to exploit the knowledge and expertise of your staff, enabling you to generate a better understanding of your organization, its ethos and its ambitions.

Maintaining goodwill

A proven commitment to keeping audiences fully informed can reap valuable rewards, especially in terms of 'goodwill'. And an organization which is not afraid to communicate during bad times as well as good can engender considerable loyalty from those most important to its ongoing success. Effective communications during less successful periods also help stifle rumour and misinformation.

Maximizing investment in other marketing activities

PR is an ideal complement to a host of other marketing initiatives, from advertising to exhibitions. It can also provide more sustained promotion of a particular marketing message, providing a platform on which other activities can ride, and making the most of the overall marketing budget.

Improving staff morale

Positive messages about one's employer can only reinforce a feeling of well-being at work – as long as the messages are accurate of course.

Good PR can impact upon staff recruitment and retention, as you find that the quality of candidates for new positions improves as the reputation of your organization is enhanced.

A positive contribution to business success

A 'favourable' image is an invaluable asset. It will encourage loyalty through bad times as well as good, and not just among customers or clients: from employees (current and potential); from financial backers, from the bank manager to shareholders; from your local community (very important if what you do has a direct impact upon their everyday lives or their environment). Of course, customers and clients are vital, as are those who might recommend your company to someone else – they all need to think well of you, to want you to succeed and to want to support you with their time or their money.

In PR, such 'general' goodwill is encouraged and fostered through a 'corporate' PR campaign (explained in more detail on page 7). The 'corporate brand' now plays an integral role in the marketing strategies of many organizations, managed primarily through the PR campaign. The corporate brand can wield considerable power and influence, and although essentially a commercial tool, it also embodies the 'personality' of the organization, over and above product or service, and emphasizes 'core values'. Consumers and others (especially shareholders) are becoming increasingly aware of corporate values, and want to ally themselves with organizations whose ethics, business approach or even politics match their own – corporate attitude towards sustainability is a particularly relevant example. Corporate PR aims to promote the brand and its values, and in doing so actively encourages long-term support and contributes to long-term business success.

What 'type' of campaign?

PR campaigns fall – very roughly – into a number of broad categories, and it's important that you appreciate the differences between them before deciding which would best suit your own organization. Remember, these categories are not mutually exclusive – most organizations run one or two campaign types in parallel, in order to meet all their objectives:

Insight

Trade PR can be very different to PR aimed at consumers, and different again from PR designed to educate or inform. Understand these differences before planning your PR campaign, and appreciate how PR can support wide-ranging strategic objectives, from increasing sales to raising awareness.

TRADE

You promote your products or services primarily (possibly even exclusively) to other businesses – the 'trade' – even though the end-user may be the consumer. A trade campaign tends to be highly targeted and operates within well-defined fields; it frequently runs in conjunction with a consumer campaign (see below) in order to achieve a 'push and pull' effect – encouraging retailers to stock your products for example, whilst also persuading consumers to go and buy them. Trade campaigns tend to focus on a narrower range of communications media – each industry has its own core trade press for example, or key trade exhibitions, and so the PR campaign can be geared to exploit these to full effect. Trade PR can also explore the possibilities offered by 'vertical markets' – markets not directly associated with your product or service but important to the audiences which you wish to influence (and for more on this, see page 137).

BUSINESS TO BUSINESS

Similar in many ways to a trade campaign, business to business PR usually describes the promotion of professional service providers – lawyers, bankers, accountants, business advisers and so on. Business to business campaigns often focus more on the demonstration of knowledge and expertise than the direct promotion of specific products or services. Many campaigns have a strong regional bias, as target audiences tend to be within the local business community, and as a result many national organizations run both local and national campaigns in order to target their audiences more effectively.

CONSUMER

This term is generally applied to any campaign aimed at 'the general public', but in fact, the public is usually segmented according to a varying set of parameters including age, sex, location, income – the list can be long and sophisticated. Most consumer campaigns demand greater resources as audiences can be very large, the variety of communication channels greater, and more creativity required in order to both attract attention and counter the activities of the competition in what could be a very crowded marketplace.

CORPORATE

As has already been mentioned, PR can also be used to maintain the reputation of your organization at a 'corporate' level, and corporate campaigns often run alongside other PR programmes to underline core values, and to provide a way of communicating general business information which is of interest to a wider range of audiences. 'Government' or 'public affairs' campaigns fall within this remit, using PR to enable the effective lobbying of key Government influencers, as does financial PR (designed to support activities related to the stock-market). See Chapter 9 for more on these two specialist areas.

ISSUE/INFORMATION

Not all PR campaigns are driven by commercial incentives. PR is used just as effectively by public bodies, charities, NGOs, campaign or pressure groups and by other not-for-profit organizations, including local clubs and societies. These organizations use PR to promote their activities, to educate or inform target audiences about new developments, or raise awareness of issues of concern among audiences of all types and from all sections of the community. Commercial organizations often use PR to do this as well, perhaps by sponsoring an information campaign, if a target audience needs to be educated as well as informed. PR can prove very effective in educational campaigns as it comprises a range of activities capable of disseminating quite complex or involved information to both very specific and wide-ranging target audiences.

A NOTE ON THE EXERCISES
IN THIS BOOK

At the end of each chapter you'll find a brief exercise (entitled 'Test yourself'), designed to test your understanding of the preceding information, and to help you create, step by step, your own PR programme by completing a 'PR Matrix'. This is a simple framework which will allow you to define and link all the various elements of a campaign to ensure that every activity is there for a purpose, and that no aims or objectives have been overlooked. As you work your way through this book, you'll learn about all the activities which could be employed within a PR campaign – if you decide that some of those suggested simply don't suit the nature of your organization, then of course don't include them in your final programme. But even so it's good to know about all the techniques you could use, in case your organization – or your job – changes in the future!

2

....

Planning a PR campaign

In this chapter you will learn:
- *how to define aims and objectives*
- *how to define target audiences*
- *more about the message and the medium*

You may think that the term 'PR campaign' is rather grand for
what you had in mind – perhaps a bit of press coverage in the local
paper, or a seminar or party for your clients or customers – but
whatever your immediate ambitions, gathering your ideas together
under the umbrella of a 'campaign' is a sensible way to begin. As
with any other marketing activity, strategic forethought is vital. PR
can take up a lot of your time and often your money, and if it's not
targeted precisely, timed effectively and executed efficiently then all
your hard work and valuable budget may go to waste. Don't try
and sketch out ideas 'when you've got a minute'. Sit down properly,
with colleagues if you think it will help, and work through the stages
outlined in this chapter. Don't forget that planning will remain a
fairly fluid process for quite a long time – you'll find that the simple
exercise of working through your thoughts may make you think
again about certain fundamental issues, but as a result you should
have a much clearer idea of what you want to do, why you'll be
doing it and what the outcome should be. In effect, you'll have
created the bones of your 'campaign'.

A NOTE ON PRODUCT AND SERVICE PR

Although there are many similarities, it's important to highlight
the differences between PR campaigns for products and services,

and to keep these in mind when starting to plan your own PR strategy.

The essential difference is tangibility. A product is there – it will be visible on a shelf, it can be photographed, it can be seen in action, its benefits can be immediately appreciated. A service does not exist until it is being executed, and therefore the invaluable tangibility has to be created in other ways.

PR is a very useful tool for the service industry, and it can be used to promote services just as effectively as products. Products tend to rise or fall on their own merits, and on the buzz which surrounds them. The importance of the manufacturer is often less to the fore, unless the name brings kudos (i.e. any designer product) or is an important part of the whole package. There are many books on product marketing which go into strategic issues in greater detail than is necessary here.

For a service company, the organization is the service – think of any bank or other high street service organization such as a travel agent or accountancy firm – and so target audiences are far more aware of an organization's reputation and history, and this affects their buying patterns and loyalties. Although services can be marketed as 'products', corporate PR plays a much more important role in any campaign for a service organization.

Defining aims and objectives

When putting together any sort of marketing plan, it's important to try and define your aims and objectives right from the start – for the purpose of this book the following definitions are used:

▶ **Aims** – *measurable ambitions*
▶ **Objectives** – *the means by which you will achieve your aims*

To take a very broad example, the reason why you're reading this book can probably be translated into the following aim:

▶ *To raise the profile of my organization*

Which can then be translated into the following objective:

▶ *To put in place a PR campaign*

Your marketing plan will have already established the overall marketing aims for your organization, and these will form the basis for your PR campaign. But make sure you don't just use PR as a dumping ground for the corporate wish list. Keep your PR aims well defined, achievable, and realistic – and this last point may demand some brute honesty about your organization or your product or service. You may think your company is the most fascinating, dynamic organization in the country and that the national press would just love to hear about you – but would they really? Is your organization that unusual? Are your products really that unique? It's not that you should undersell yourself, but PR is an activity which demands truth (despite what you may have heard), and creating unreasonable, unsustainable hype will not do you any favours in the long run.

Also make sure that the aims you establish are measurable (in some form or another), otherwise, how else can you evaluate them? It's easy to say that your aim is 'to become the best-known design agency in Newcastle', or 'to become leaders in the field of brewing technology', but such statements come apart very quickly under scrutiny. How would you define 'best-known' for example? What exactly is a 'leader in the field'? How can you find out when you've become the 'best-known' or the 'leader'?

Your aims and objectives will also establish the practical parameters of your campaign, the geographical scope for example, timescale and other such factors. It's also very important to remember that PR cannot achieve all your marketing ambitions for you. It will be working in tandem with a number of other marketing activities which will – together – help you to achieve your corporate ambitions. Therefore, tease out those results which PR can realistically hope to accomplish.

Insight

When defining a PR campaign, first establish measurable aims and then translate these into tangible objectives, the activities employed to achieve your aims. Use your marketing strategy to inform your PR planning, and to place PR in the context of your other marketing activities.

Let's consider an example, in order to put these thoughts into perspective.

A growing and ambitious company manufactures, among other products, Klipp'ems, a revolutionary new re-usable staple, destined – the MD is sure – to revolutionize the lives of office staff everywhere. Having drafted a marketing strategy, the Marketing Director has jotted down the aims which he hopes his PR campaign will achieve:

▶ *To let everyone know about the Klipp'ems system.*
▶ *To make Klipp'ems the 'number one' brand of paper fastener.*

Examined closely, these aims are rather breathtaking – to let everyone know? Everyone in the country, or in the whole world? And to make Klipp'ems the 'number one' brand – what market share would they need in order to achieve this? How many Klipp'ems units would they have to sell? Do they even manufacture this amount? How quickly would they have to grow in order to realize this ambition? How long are we talking about in order to achieve this – a year? A decade? And how do we know when it's happened?

Admittedly, these are only first thoughts, but it does save time if you can apply more discipline to the process right from the start.

So let's see if we can re-draft these thoughts into more realistic PR aims – for example:

> ▶ *To promote the Klipp'ems system to our main target customer groups in selected regions – those identified as having maximum potential for growth*
> ▶ *To contribute towards a growth rate of 10% per year for nationwide sales, in order to gain 20% of the paper fastener market within 10 years*

As you can see, the aims are now anchored to some practical facts and figures – and although, no doubt, these will be revisited and probably revised as time passes, at least we have a strategic direction in which to go. The sales team have also attached some hard figures to the aim of becoming 'number one' – they've decided, realistically, how much of the existing market they can hope to penetrate, given current and future manufacturing capacity and staffing levels, and defined a timescale in which to achieve that goal. Using terms such as 'contribute' is also practical – as we've already noted, PR will be one of the many tools used to achieve such global aims, and it's important to acknowledge this up front.

Objectives, as we said earlier, are the practical means by which you will achieve your aims, and at this stage it's only necessary to sketch in the broadest possible detail, once again in order to give strategic direction for the next stage of the planning process. So in response to the aims, the objectives can be defined as:

> ▶ *To establish a PR campaign which will:*
>   ▷ *Raise awareness, in key regions and nationwide, of the Klipp'ems brand.*
>   ▷ *Educate potential users about the new system. Generate quality leads.*

These key objectives define the main campaign drivers: that there are a number of groups of people which need to know about the Klipp'ems system; that these can be defined geographically; and that there is an educational as well as a selling job to be done.

Defining your target audience

Now that you have outlined your aims and objectives – why and how you want to use PR – you can start to consider your target audiences, the people with whom you want to communicate.

Who is most important to your success? Think carefully, because this list could stretch well beyond current and potential customers. Consider the following groups and identify those of most relevance to you – and don't forget to define criteria such as geographical spread or industry sector for each different group. You may end up with a long list but still decide only to direct your PR towards one or two specific groups, which is a perfectly valid strategy, and may be more realistic if your budget is limited or you are just starting to explore the potential of PR.

Your list will probably include:

CUSTOMERS OR CLIENTS

This category is probably top of most lists, but rather than being lumped together as one homogenous group, consider sub-dividing them further into former, current and potential customers, as you may need a different strategy for each. For example, former customers need to know about new products or services which could entice them back; helping to maintain the loyalty of existing clients may be an important issue, particularly if they need reassurance that they made the right choice (especially related to high-ticket items), or if recommendation plays an important role in the purchasing decision and they could recommend you to someone else; and how can you convert a potential into a current customer?

If you are launching a consumer campaign, then you need to closely define your customers or clients in order to enable activities to be planned efficiently, as consumer audiences can range enormously in size and characteristics. When planning a trade campaign, as well as identifying the type of client or customer you want to target (probably in the broad terms of their business or activity) it's also important to identify more precisely those job functions within each target organization which are most important to you, and these will probably be at a number of levels. Although your service or product may be desired on the shop floor, for example, it might be the Finance Director who needs to be convinced to spend the money. Likewise, your product may be designed to help a specific team within a company, but the credibility of your organization – its financial stability, for example, or wider reputation – may need to be proven to the Board of Directors first before your solution is adopted.

'INTERESTED GROUPS'

If you are using PR to promote an issue – rather than to develop a business or service – then you'll need to identify the type of people that you need to target, grouping them by those criteria which will help focus your campaign activities – by location, for example, income, sex, association with a particular event. Look at the ideas for clients and customers as many them are also relevant here. Who is already interested? How can you keep them up to speed? Who has lost interest – can you get them back on board? Who should be informed but isn't?

DISTRIBUTORS OR AGENTS

This refers to anyone selling your products or services on your behalf. If you don't sell directly to your customers then you need to ensure that whoever does is both the target of and supported by your PR campaign, in order to encourage and help them to work harder on your behalf. Direct promotion of your products or services will also improve market conditions for your distributors, and may even increase competition between those distributors who actively want to represent you.

A note on OEMs

If you are an OEM – an Original Equipment Manufacturer – then you will be selling on to other organizations who will use your products (perhaps as a component, an ingredient or as part of a fabric, for example). Your PR planning may be limited just to those likely to buy your products, but if your product is a selling point in itself then you may want to extend your PR to end users, whether they are trade or consumer. This will in turn support both your sales and the sales of your primary customers.

SUPPLIERS

Add these to your list if you are heavily dependent upon their goodwill and support through bad times as well as good. Being perceived as a good customer, especially if your business is clearly growing successfully, will also result in fiercer competition for your business.

INFLUENCERS AND ADVISERS

This term embraces anyone who may recommend your organization to other target audiences on your list. The nature of the individuals within this group is often quite specific to a particular business. For example, speaking from my own experience, PR consultants are often recommended by designers, advertising agencies and marketing agencies, and also by business advisers – government-funded business agencies, for example, banks or even accountants. In other professions, trade associations can be very influential, or associated or complementary organizations. Think laterally and you may discover that this target audience is more extensive than you think, and also very important.

FINANCIAL SECTOR

Even the smallest business may need financial support of some kind, and good PR can help reassure your backers that you are really doing well and deserve ongoing support. As an organization grows, it may need to attract additional funding, so investors or shareholders should be added to the list in due course.

THE LOCAL COMMUNITY

If your organization operates purely on a local level then this is obviously a key audience, but using PR to maintain a good relationship with your local community can be beneficial in other ways. It can help attract a better quality of staff, for example, and if your organization has a physical impact upon the local environment – perhaps you operate a manufacturing plant, or have a large site within a town – then this becomes even more important, especially if you have plans to expand.

MEMBERS

If your organization is run by or for a membership body, then your members (past, current and potential) are among the most important audiences for your PR campaign. Depending on their relationship with the organization, the membership can be a demanding audience, and one which can require regular communication in order to reassure them that their membership fees are being well spent. Context is everything here – members of a professional body, for example, have a real stake in the success of the organization as that success could directly affect their professional status, and so they may need a very specific PR campaign geared to their expectations. Members of a local wildlife group, however, may consider their membership fee as being a charitable donation, and are therefore happy if communications are relatively infrequent.

YOUR STAFF

We look at internal PR in more detail in Chapter 7, but suffice to say that your staff should not be neglected when planning your PR campaign. Informed staff feel valued and respected, and a robust system of communication also keeps the effects of a damaging rumour-mill to a minimum.

Insight

Target audiences can range far wider than you might originally think, so be creative when defining those groups with whom you currently communicate, whether you 'talk' to them every day, or hardly ever. Geographical spread and industry sector are also important for each audience.

So try to be creative when listing your audiences – once again, think laterally and use as broad a brush as possible. This is the list, jotted down in no particular order, that the Klipp'ems team has come up with:

- ▶ *Office workers*
- ▶ *PAs/admin teams*
- ▶ *Office managers – department heads*
- ▶ *Home office – teleworkers/self-employed/leisure*
- ▶ *Stationery suppliers (shops, catalogues)*
- ▶ *Gift shops?*
- ▶ *Schools/colleges – students*
- ▶ *Bank/accountant*
- ▶ *Klipp'ems reps*
- ▶ *Staff*

Let's take another example, this time looking at a service-based organization. The Clean Sweeps provide contract cleaning services to both private homes and offices in and around a small town, targeting anyone who needs a regular cleaner, or a one-off blitz. Not only do they want to expand their portfolio of regular clients, but they also need to constantly recruit cleaners for their books – in fact, keeping cleaners is a problem they want to try and address, and so they've made this one of their main aims. Target audiences in this case have been defined and divided as follows:

Customers
- ▶ *Busy home-owners (i.e. working full-time)*
- ▶ *House-movers*
- ▶ *Office managers*
- ▶ *Landlords/estate agents*

Advisers
- ▶ *Local business advisers (i.e. Chambers of Commerce)*
- ▶ *Other cleaning services (i.e. window cleaning/facilities management) staff*
- ▶ *Local people looking for part-time employment*
- ▶ *Job centres and employment advisers*
- ▶ *Existing staff*

As you can see, although it's easy to think that you should only try and attract the attention of your customer, there are a whole range of audiences vital to the ongoing success of your organization, and your PR campaign should make sure that communications are maintained with every relevant group.

Audience, message and medium

Now that you know to whom you want to talk, the next stage is to decide what to say – the message – and to identify the best way of saying it – the medium.

MESSAGES

Messages are exactly that. The translation of your aims and objectives into messages specific to each individual audience, which they will understand and to which you hope they will respond appropriately. Defining the 'message' is not supposed to be an exercise in 'spin', designed to distort or hide reality, but more a means of establishing 'what does this person need to know, what do I want this person to know, and how should I tell him?'

Let's look at an example, once again from the Klipp'ems campaign. The Klipp'ems team sees 'office workers' as a key target group, and wants to persuade more of them to adopt the Klipp'ems system. Messages for this audience will of course include the more obvious, such as:

> ▶ 'Klipp'ems is a system which will really benefit my working life', and
> ▶ 'Klipp'ems is a much improved alternative to traditional staples because ...'

But PR also encourages the promotion of more subtle messages such as:

> 'Klipp'ems comes from a growing company which has an
> exciting future – if my whole office changes to Klipp'ems, then
> I will still be able to use the system in 10 years' time.'

Here are some more examples. Klipp'ems are going to be sold primarily through stationery shops, and so retailers are a prime target. Messages will therefore range from:

> ▶ 'Klipp'ems is an exciting new brand of paper fastener.'
> to:
> ▶ 'Customers choosing Klipp'ems will return to me for top-up
>   supplies thus generating extra business.'
> to:
> ▶ 'Klipp'ems will be backed by an extensive advertising campaign,
>   ensuring my stock will sell fast.'

The Clean Sweeps have identified recruitment as a key problem area, so they have decided that their PR programme must include the following messages wherever possible:

> ▶ Clean Sweeps is a good employer, with a good reputation.
> ▶ Clean Sweeps offers services of the highest quality – only
>   the best cleaning staff are employed.

Go through all your audience groups one by one and list all the key messages which you need to get across – you'll probably find that many are common to a number groups, especially those which focus on your organization rather than on a specific product or service, so your final list will be more manageable than you may initially fear.

Remember that although messages are essentially substantive – providing the text or sub-text for an actual activity – they can also act as strategic guidelines, helping you decide which activities to pursue (which we look at in more detail in the following section). For example, the Clean Sweeps have listed 'We are an excellent local employer' as one of their messages. If they can publicize any good stories about recruitment – perhaps that they've just employed 20 new cleaners for example – then such news is an ideal vehicle for the message they have identified. However, if they were invited to speak on the problems of recruitment at a national employers conference, tempting though the offer might be, they should perhaps turn it down. The conference audience would not be local, would be very unlikely to become a Clean Sweeps client or cleaner, and the emphasis is on a problem rather than success – the opposite of their defined message.

MEDIUM/ACTIVITY

The medium – or activity – is the method you choose of getting each message across to the target audience. PR is primarily thought of as a press-based activity – using the media to publicize your news – and 'media liaison' is still very much the bread and butter of many PR campaigns. But PR encourages versatility, and there are many other ways of getting a message across, as you will discover as you work your way through the rest of this book.

It's important to keep in mind the fundamental nature of each audience when considering this element of campaign planning. What are the main characteristics of this group – are they geographically widespread for example, or concentrated locally? Are they a small group or do they number in thousands? And – most important of all – what are the most effective means of communication when talking to this target group?

If your audience is geographically widespread, and numerically potentially unlimited (as for, say a consumer campaign for chocolate), then a wide-ranging media campaign may well be a good way to start, in order to achieve extensive nationwide coverage. But if your audience is either very small or very discrete, and your message very specific or complex then a media campaign may too broad-brush, too transitory or too superficial, to have the desired effect. A seminar or social event may be more effective, or a directly mailed newsletter or ezine may be a more cost-effective means of achieving the desired result.

The PR audit

Most organizations don't start their PR plan with a clean sheet.
They've already been practising PR, perhaps in an ad hoc way, for
many years or they have already gained some publicity without
really trying, perhaps because they have grown spectacularly
quickly. Other organizations may find themselves with a history
of mixed PR which has left target audiences with impressions
which are no longer true – this may the case for an organization
which suffered a major trauma, for example (such as a major
accident – there will be more on crisis PR in Chapter 8). But this
can also be the case for an organization with a long history – a
local school, for example, or a government body. If you are such
an organization (but even if you're not), then it may be worth
implementing a PR audit right at the start of your campaign.

A PR audit is a way of finding out exactly what your ad hoc (and
other, more sustained) PR activities have achieved in terms of your
reputation, awareness of products or services, and your ranking
against competitors or other similar organizations, and what (if
any) residual perceptions still remain. PR audits are also useful for
those organizations who wish to ramp up their PR programme,
and want guidance on the best direction in which to go, or for
those who feel their PR has stagnated, and need to know why.

PR audits tend to be qualitative rather than quantitative pieces of
research: in other words, rather than questioning large numbers
of relevant people (your customers for example), fewer, but more
influential or representative individuals are targeted and usually
asked more in-depth questions. For example, an influential

journalist on a key trade paper could give very interesting insights on your reputation within the media; a management consultant may also be able to speak for a great number of clients on issues such as reputation and standing; and the leader of a relevant society (a users' group, for example, or a special interest body) could talk on behalf of a whole swathe of customers.

In a perfect world, the audit should be carried out before a PR campaign has been launched and then repeated after it has been completed or has been running for a set period of time. But in reality few organizations have the budget to carry out such research on a regular basis – and the impact of a PR campaign can be measured reasonably effectively in other ways (see Chapter 11). But even if an audit is only carried out once in a blue moon, it can still provide invaluable reassurance that the PR programme is on track, or show that certain audiences need to be addressed in a different way, and it will also give a unique snapshot of the marketplace in which your PR programme has to be effective. It can also reveal where audiences diverge (which often happens when an organization wants to change a brand, or modernize its image), and if differences of opinion emerge, making you choose which group you really want to appeal to most.

If you plan to undergo such an exercise, keep your questionnaire as short and to the point as possible, and suitable for a telephone interview. You can either reveal your organization's name at the beginning, the middle or at the end of the exercise – if you are already quite well known then hiding behind anonymity for at least part of the interview may help increase the honesty of the answers you receive. If you are relatively unknown, then you'll lose nothing by identifying yourselves up front. Most audits go for a half and half approach – asking general questions first, then identifying the originator of the audit before moving on to more specific questions about reputation and so on.

When thinking about your questionnaire, make sure you address issues such as the most widely respected media (press, broadcast, internet) for each audience; the way target groups gain different types of information (including social media); the reputation of your organization (couched in terms relevant and meaningful to your aims i.e. reliable, honest, fast-growing, fly-by-night), and the way you are perceived when compared to other organizations, both competitor and complementary. Specific questions will depend greatly upon the nature of your target audiences and the status you have already gained. Your main aim is to gain a picture of what PR has achieved for you so far, and where the best opportunities now lie.

Ideally you should get professional help when drafting your questionnaire, and even to implement the survey itself. Telephone interviews – even when the target list is reasonably limited – can prove very time consuming, and you'll want to complete the exercise in as short a timescale as possible in order to gather an accurate snapshot of the situation at a particular time. Market research specialists and PR professionals will both be able to help. Of course, you will still have to provide a list of contacts to interview, drawn from each of your target audiences. To get a good end result, try to generate a list comprising both those who you know are familiar with your organization and those totally unknown to you, possibly amending the questionnaire to reflect any obvious differences between the two groups. Familiar contacts may even be warned that the survey will take place, 'warming them up' in advance so that they are both more receptive to the questionnaire, and have thought about what they might say.

If your budget is restricted, or the questions you've identified are quite limited (such as a focus only on the most read publications, or most viewed websites), then you may be able to tack the audit onto the back of another market research exercise – even if it's just a case of adding a few quick questions to a customer satisfaction form – or send it out as an email, asking individuals to respond the same way.

Timing

When is the best time to launch your campaign? Is the season important (as it is, say, in the agricultural, health or gardening industries)? Is there a major industry event, such as a trade fair, which would provide a good focus for your campaign launch, or would you in fact prefer to wait until the show is over and everyone is looking for something new? Do your clients have well-known financial markers – say a common end of year – which may result in higher or lower spending? Are January and September the best dates (these are frequently cited as good times of year, being the return from major holiday periods)? How does your timing translate overseas, if your audiences are spread around the globe?

The timing of each individual PR activity is also important – some will need to be regular in order to maintain impact (the generation of press coverage, for example, or the issue of a newsletter or ezine). Some activities will work better as a one-off (special events for example), and others are designed specifically to deliver more sustained results, such as a sponsorship programme. Once you have identified the most important regular dates in your PR calendar, then make sure your additional activities – if you have any left! – are evenly spaced throughout the rest of the year, in order to maintain an even flow of information going out to your target groups, and also to avoid stressing your PR team too much! For example, some will be seasonal (outdoor events, or those linked to a specific holiday); some will have to tie in with the calendar of the target audience (to focus on a particular trade exhibition, etc.); some may take advantage of an external initiative – a national campaign day for example. Activities also have specific lead times, and these need to be appreciated well in advance, if deadlines – and opportunities – are not to be missed.

A useful aim may be to ensure one PR activity is completed every month, and this may range from a simple press release to support for that major exhibition stand. Treating PR planning almost mechanically means that the momentum is maintained – you may find that some months need no thought, while at other times you're scrabbling around for something to say, but momentum is important in PR so it is worth making the effort to sustain it. Having said that, there will be key times in some industries where very little is going on; in the education sector, for example, exam time and main holidays are always quiet, although it may still be worth targeting those other audiences who are still around – advisers, parents, suppliers and so on.

A final point – the timing of your campaign will also influence the nature of the PR team which you put together (see the next section, and Chapter 10, for more on this). If you know that you'll only ever be doing one or two main activities a year, then you can create a flexible team comprising part-time, in-house and external help. If the campaign is to be long-term and sustained, then the creation of a dedicated team, or the employment of a full-time PRO (Public Relations Officer) is more logical, and will also underline the commitment to PR that you, as an organization, is making.

Insight

Good PR is the result of good management and effective evaluation, so don't scrimp on resources. You'll need people who can be proactive as well as reactive, highly efficient administrators, and creative thinkers. You'll also need to keep excellent records in order to evaluate successfully.

Managing a PR campaign

You may have pinned down your audiences, refined your messages and identified a range of activities, but there are still some important details – both strategic and administrative – to be put in place before you can start.

STAFF AND RESOURCES

If PR remains constantly at the bottom of your list of things to do, then it will never be effective or deliver real results. You'll always be reacting to events, never making the most of upcoming opportunities, and constantly feel that things could be handled better – especially when you see what your competitors have achieved. Good PR is a balance of pro- and reactive activities and so your PR campaign, and the resources supporting it, should be capable of managing both.

PR needs dedicated time, both for planning and for implementation, and the amount of time needed depends, of course, on the scope of your plans. Once you have decided on the PR activities that will best achieve your aims you can then estimate how much time will be needed to fulfil your ambitions, and plan your staffing arrangements accordingly.

When it comes to running a PR campaign, there are a number of options: using in-house personnel, either full or part time; employing a PR agency or freelance consultant; or using a mixture of the two. In Chapter 10 we look in more detail at the dynamics of a PR team, and also at what PR professionals can offer and how they should be used. Remember, you'll probably need assistance on two levels – strategic and administrative. Despite the excellent advice given in this book, you probably need specialist help at some level to help you steer your campaign through its first few months using either a consultant, or exploiting in-house expertise on a formal basis. Depending on the activity, PR can also be highly labour intensive so make sure you have someone on the PR team able to handle database and contact management, and record keeping. If you are planning any sort of major event, you'll also need to identify willing hands able to help out when needed.

ONGOING REVIEW AND EVALUATION

Once again, this topic has been given a chapter to itself, but it deserves to be mentioned here because it will influence the way you set up and run your PR campaign.

As your campaign proceeds, you should be constantly reviewing and re-evaluating the essential elements which are in play – and Chapter 11 demonstrates how this can be done. Practically, this demands that the PR team meets at appropriate intervals to both review what's going on, evaluate results, and to brainstorm new ideas. Regular meetings also allow you to consider new opportunities which have arisen since you started planning your campaign – or new threats. PR should always remain a flexible resource; there will always be set activities which will dominate your PR strategy – major trade exhibitions for example, or product launches – but around these, you should attempt to be as proactive as possible. Brainstorming sessions are also an opportunity for other members of your organization to get involved. They may not understand the mechanics of PR, but they may still be able to provide new ideas and angles on what can be done, and identify new opportunities. It's also important to remember that PR is a service for the organization as a whole, and should remain responsive to the needs of all employees.

TEST YOURSELF

A new 'Environmental Centre' is being set up in a local town. It hopes to provide information on all aspects of 'low carbon lifestyles', and will sell sustainable products both in its shop and its own café. It also hopes to act as a catalyst for changing public opinion locally, while contributing to the national debate. The Centre managers are now beginning to sketch out a PR programme. What are the Centre's PR aims, and how can they be translated into realistic objectives? Which target audiences should they list? And what do they want to say to each one?

PR Matrix

You could sketch out your answers to the exercise above by starting a PR Matrix – and then start to draft one for your own organization. Your first action is, of course, to establish your aims and objectives and then complete the first two columns of your matrix, heading these 'target audience' and 'main messages', making sure there are no gaps. If your aims are wide ranging then you may find that you have to create a number of different matrices and develop discrete programmes, but make sure they are integrated into the overall campaign.

3

Media liaison

In this chapter you will learn:
- *how to identify your target media*
- *more about social media*
- *different ways to let the media know about you*
- *what to do about 'bad press'*
- *about press photography*

'Media liaison' often plays the leading role within a PR programme (both in its own right, and in support of other activities), and may in fact be the only activity that an organization wants to implement. The term is used to describe the structured approach to gaining relevant, quality coverage in the media – print, broadcast, online (both those with print equivalents and independent), and social media. It embraces both the proactive – issuing press releases and so on – and the reactive, and although the focus of such a campaign is usually the promotion of stories about your organization, media coverage can also be given to events and other activities specially created to generate 'news'.

A media campaign has to be planned meticulously, and sustained over the long term if good results are to be achieved. The press will rarely come rushing to your door unless you have something absolutely staggering to say (or are embroiled in a crisis), and so you have to be the one who creates the opportunities. A lot of time and energy can be spent trying to gain media coverage, with little to show for it at the end. This chapter explains how to start planning your media campaign, and how to make sure you maximize your chances of success.

Determining what 'success' represents is key. The ultimate goal is to gain good exposure in the right vehicle, even though this cannot always be guaranteed – and strategies must also be put in place to deal with any negative coverage you might receive. The breadth of your media liaison programme depends greatly upon the size of your organization, and upon the quality and nature of the information you can supply. Of course, the bigger or more influential you are, the more you become news in your own right, and therefore have to be prepared to monitor, analyse and respond to coverage on an almost daily basis.

For the vast majority of organizations, media liaison is mainly proactive, undertaken because media coverage is often considered to be very important, especially if one's main rival has just been featured in a key publication! A good feature in an important magazine, for example, is often considered by a target audience as an independent, informed endorsement of your product or organization and can therefore carry a value that far exceeds the results of any other type of marketing activity. But media liaison can also be very unpredictable and for that reason is usually only one element within the PR mix. But if it is, nevertheless, an important part, then how do you maximize your chances of success?

Identifying your target media

Your first job is to identify the media in which you would like to gain coverage. Look back at your list of target audiences and work from there, thinking of the type of media each audience would read, watch, follow, log on or listen to. Don't try to be too specific at this stage – we're simply trying to identify some basic categories – and once again, think creatively and as broadly as possible.

Listed below are some of the most easily identifiable categories to get you started, and ways of refining these categories further. Remember that you don't have to include all these categories on your media list, tempting though it might be – only choose those which you know cover stories about the activities of an organization such as yours, and which, of course, are read by your target audiences. You can always expand the list on an ad hoc basis if you suddenly have a story which you know is of wider interest. The structure of your list also depends upon the geographical scope of your campaign. At the moment, we're really only dealing with 'domestic' media – you may have to repeat the exercise country by country if you are planning a major international campaign.

So, consider the following:

PRINT MEDIA

National daily and weekly newspapers and news magazines
Consider which correspondents would be most interested in what you're doing (i.e. science and technology, lifestyle, business) or if you only want to contact the newsdesk; you could also find out about local 'stringers' – journalists based in your area who pick up on stories and forward them to the national media (and a local PR consultancy can help you here, as part of their services).

Regional daily and weekly newspapers (including freesheets)
Although increasingly threatened by the internet, regional publications still number in their hundreds, so if you plan to target them, break down your selection by specific region or by circulation (to identify the most widely read publications in each area) in order to generate a more manageable list.

Consumer publications
This term refers to those publications aimed at the 'general public', including general interest titles (i.e. 'lifestyle', or monthly women's magazines) and the more specific (such as sport, food or hobby magazines), for all age groups and for all stages of life. If this category is relevant to your PR campaign, segment it

carefully – you want to be able to manage both the dispatch and the response involved in tackling this significant media sector. Also, as you will already know from your own experience, consumer titles can come and go very quickly and so this category needs regular review if it is important to your overall strategy.

Industry-specific trade publications

Every industry has at least one or two publications which are read by everyone, and many are well known outside their industry as key barometers of industry developments, opinion and trends. You need to identify the key publications for each industry sector you wish to target – ask some members of your target audiences to provide guidelines if you don't already know. Circulation numbers can provide another indicator, but only up to a certain point. Some subscription-only publications, with quite a limited circulation, can prove to be the most influential. Sometimes, general press release coverage is charged for in these publications, so be prepared to make a contribution if you really want to be featured regularly in key media – and remember that it will be significantly less than if you advertise.

General business publications

Certain business publications – especially those aimed at management level staff – are read across all industry sectors, and can be very influential. Regional business magazines and newspapers can also be well read, and can prove useful if you are marketing at a local level. However, they usually only cover news about organizations in their area, so only contact those outside your own region if you can demonstrate a strong local connection.

Society and association newsletters and magazines (both professional and amateur)

Most professional organizations (such as trade associations or professional bodies), and larger societies publish their own newsletters and magazines, many very influential in their own right, and so should be included if relevant; likewise many less formal associations (amateur associations, clubs or special interest groups) have regular newsletters, which could prove a valuable addition to your list if you have a product or service particularly relevant to a niche audience.

Commercial publications and magazines

Supermarkets, banks, department stores, insurance companies – many now publish quite sophisticated magazines which are often distributed free to customers. Many accept unsolicited press material from outside their own organization, as it is important that the editorial appears at least semi-independent.

BROADCAST MEDIA

National and local radio and TV

Identify those programmes or (perhaps more specialist) channels which may pick up on your news, or which will be interested more generally in your organization and what it does (feature programmes, special interest programmes etc.); if you want to target newsdesks, then once again try to identify the most relevant correspondent, or find local stringers who can work on your behalf.

If you feel TV coverage, in particular, is essential to your PR strategy (rather than the icing on the cake) then you need to look closely at all relevant opportunities and work out ways in which you can provide content which a TV journalist or producer will actively want. Identify all the different programmes which might be interested in what you have to offer (you could use a professional PR agency to help you), and which will reach your target audiences – this will lead you to the many and varied production companies currently working in TV, many of which specialize in certain programme types. A word of warning: getting coverage on TV can be very time-consuming, with results of very varied quality, so only pursue this route if you consider TV coverage crucial to your TV campaign. For more on how to get TV coverage, see page 67.

When considering radio, then there are again hundreds of options (even more so when digital radio is added to the mix) from the very local to the international. If radio coverage is a key part of your campaign, then you may also need professional help to identify all the possible stations you could target, their listener demographics and the best programmes to go for. For more on radio coverage see also page 67.

> ## Insight
> With so many different types of media, it's easy to create an impossibly long list of likely media targets. To refine your research, start by asking target audiences about the media they read, listen to, watch or bookmark to gain a picture of where you need to be featured.

SOCIAL MEDIA

Social media is the term used to refer to any form of online activity which allows users to interact with each other, perhaps by giving opinion, inviting comment, sharing knowledge, or just socializing online. Although not a 'traditional' media liaison tool (compared to, say, direct contact with a magazine), the lines between categories are becoming increasingly blurred, and it is included in this chapter because it has the power to reach so many people, and because it is often monitored very closely by journalists.

At the time of writing, widely used social media tools include blogs, twitter, social networking and video sharing websites, podcasts, vodcasts, wikis, Q&A sites and forums – just to name a few, and by the time you read this, this list will probably have changed, if not in category but in priority, and with new technologies extending choice even further. Websites are, of course, the home for most social media, but we'll look in more detail at websites in Chapter 4, where they are treated as more of a 'static' rather than an interactive resource.

Social media is becoming an increasingly important PR tool, as it offers the potential to reach huge audiences very quickly, and this can open up exciting possibilities for many organizations, bringing access to markets or audiences previously impossible to reach, and helping build communities of supportive individuals – whether this means they respect your brand, want to buy your products, support your cause, or are just keen to hear more about what you're up to every day. Social media is therefore very enticing for anyone with global ambitions and limited budgets, and can also prove very effective in niche marketing, as it offers a means for likeminded individuals to find each other – wherever in the world they may be – and then to find, and recommend to others, the services, products or organizations they want to support.

But this global reach also makes social media a vehicle which needs skill to manage and monitor effectively, and so if it is to play an important role in your PR campaign, it may be worth hiring expert advice, not least because it is an environment which is evolving very rapidly. This section deliberately, therefore, does not deal with specifics which are likely to fall out of favour as quickly as they rise in prominence (apart from blogging – dealt with under 'online media' – as a number of blogs have become well established as leading opinion-forming mechanisms).

So if social media is to feature in your PR campaign you need to have a clear strategy about what to use, how to use it, who is able to use it (and employee guidelines for the use of social media in general is no bad thing) and predetermined measures of success. By examining some of the key, emerging characteristics of social media, you can start to judge whether it is relevant to your PR campaign, and if it is, start to decide how it could be used:

A focus on opinion, advice and information: With opinion and thought the main form of currency, 'news' (in the sense of a press release) is less important than advice, understanding or knowledge (in fact, anything which your target audience could actively value). This makes it ideal for promoting a specific issue or campaign, for example, but possibly less so for other industry sectors, unless your products, services or brand is backed by a strong set of values or beliefs which you are actively keen to promote, and be associated with.

A focus on the individual: Following on from the above, a focus on thought and opinion also often results in a focus on the individual. If your organization operates in an industry where personal contact is important (any service business for example), then using social media to promote individuals could be useful. If not – and if, in fact, personal promotion is frowned upon – then it might be less relevant, except in those situations where specific expertise should be showcased.

Informality: The informal nature encouraged by much social media suits some organizations better than others, and so again only choose those tools which suit your voice, your brand and the personality of your organization. By the same token, social media can help give what may be a faceless organization some personality, so could be used if you want to change your image, or reach a new audience, especially in terms of improving accessibility. This informality, however, can be dangerous, and can encourage the 'throw away' remark which would never have reached the outside world if filtered through the normal PR scrutiny – and which could then be replicated worldwide. For this reason, social media should be treated with care and caution, and clear protocols put in place for how it should be used, both in the context of PR and beyond. With so many staff members using social media within their private lives, it's also easy to forget where the boundaries lie, and the risk of reputational damage is real, if staff members forget that their comments can be read by a much wider audience.

Also be careful when using music, images or any 'apparently' freely available source within your social media output, as you could fall foul of intellectual property and copyright laws.

Constant attention required: Your social media output will require constant updating if it is to remain of value – in other words, relevant, immediate and up to date. No wonder so many journalists become addicted to various social media tools, as they feed directly into a growing hunger for 24 hour news, and immediate coverage of breaking events.

However, even if you don't (or can't) provide a minute by minute update, you will still have to provide a fairly constant stream of material in order to meet the expectations of target audiences, and encourage them to come back for more. You need to make sure that you can supply a regular stream of content (there is nothing worse than, say, a blog last updated months ago), but set realistic ambitions for your social media activities, to stop them overtaking your core activities. Social media can easily become a drain on resources, as staff feel honour bound (or become addicted to) providing a regular flow of information, and then have to deal with the feedback received.

You'll also need to regularly monitor any comment your activities are generating (and evaluate the success of what you're doing), but the time required to do this may undermine the initial attraction of social media as a relatively cheap means of reaching some key target audiences. However, it is important. If no one comments, or only friends and family, you may want to rethink your activities. But if your material 'goes viral' (admittedly rare, but it can happen) resulting in massive attention internationally, you may have to be prepared to handle any fall out. Once again, you may benefit from expert help when planning your monitoring and evaluation activities.

Important to specific demographic groups: Certain demographic groups – especially younger people – have embraced social media and see it as a fundamental part of their daily lives. Others, especially those who rarely use a computer (and there are some), find it irrelevant, possibly even irritating. Careful analysis of the social media expectations of your target groups is therefore a basic requirement before you launch into social media in a big way.

ONLINE MEDIA

Online media agencies
The 'wire' of old, these are primarily news-based services, with in-house journalists feeding stories by the hour to newsrooms on daily and weekly national and regional media, so only include them if you plan to issue highly topical news stories with widespread appeal or interest, perhaps as a result of a launch event. These agencies also often offer a range of other PR-related services, so

may be worth investigating as part of your general PR research, if you feel you may need more support with your media campaign.

Online magazines/websites for print and broadcast media

Almost every publication, radio programme or TV show has its own website, many of which may offer opportunities for media coverage in addition to those offered in print or broadcast. For many publications, the online team may be different to the team handling the printed version, so research contact details carefully.

Online magazines

The web is now home to many internet-only magazines, both those who started out online and those which are the digital presence for a magazine no longer available in print. These magazines may appear as a website, or as a digitally enhanced facsimile of a print version, complete with pages to turn, but with multiple layers of detail on each 'page'. You need to research carefully, using your target audiences as a starting point, to see which titles are worth approaching with editorial content.

Blogs

As one of the first social media tools, the blog has established such a universal presence that it has now become an 'official' media liaison target, with influential bloggers having equivalent status to influential journalists. If there are specific blogs which are widely read in your industry, then at the very least you should be monitoring what is being said, and contribute appropriately. But be careful. Most bloggers pride themselves on their independence, and if they take against an organization – for whatever reason – they will be happy to express their dislike in their blog for all their followers to read at their leisure. As for all social media activity – take specialist advice before you commit any resources to this area of activity.

OTHER CONTACTS

Freelance journalists

Many journalists, throughout the media, are freelancers often specializing in a certain field. Find out the names of those relevant to your campaign, as they are often looking for good contacts, especially if you can provide material which will help them sell their services.

'Vertical media'

As well as the 'core' media, those media of most relevance to your target audiences, also think about 'vertical media' – this term describes those publications, programmes or online opportunities which, although not of central interest to your target, may also be influential. For example, if you are promoting a consultancy service to senior managers in the textile industry, then obviously you'll be targeting textile industry media covering industry developments – but don't forget management and business magazines as well. If you are promoting a revolutionary flea collar, then obviously you'll be targeting magazines and programmes for pet lovers – but don't forget 'lifestyle' media, where pet ownership is one of the many topics regularly covered. By looking at your target groups in this way you'll be able to expand your list, and hopefully increase your media exposure.

Insight

You need to know what your target media is interested in, and how they want to receive your information. If media liaison is an ongoing and vital PR activity, then research your list carefully, and keep it up to date. For one-off media distribution, consider using a specialist agency.

CREATING A MEDIA LIST

Once you've identified the categories most relevant to your campaign, the next stage is to home in on specific targets, and start to create a 'media distribution list'. You'll need to create a database comprising the contact details for all your targets, and you may have to do some online research, and some ringing around to find out the best person to send your information to. Most, if not all, of the media you'll want to target will have a website, so the best way to compile your list is to visit the site and find out how they prefer to receive information. Data protection laws regarding 'business' databases vary around the world, so make sure your databases comply with local regulations.

This type of research is fairly manageable if your target media are easily identifiable (e.g. architectural magazines), or the range is fairly small (e.g. daily newspapers within a specific geographical region). However, if your list is likely to be long, if it could vary widely with each press release (the case with many consumer products), stray into areas with which you are unfamiliar, or if it could be international, then it may be more cost-effective to use professional help from a news distribution agency or PR consultancy. This may seem expensive, but if you are already investing in a PR campaign, then scrimping on distribution is a false economy. Of course, many agencies are capable of handling the entire media liaison process, from writing your release to monitoring its use, and if you only plan to distribute information once or twice a year, or are planning a one-off mailing to a very extensive audience, then their services can prove relatively cost-effective, certainly saving you the effort of research and updating. For more on external PR assistance, see page 162.

Creating a media list – even a relatively limited one – can take a lot of time, and so it's important that this time isn't wasted by allowing the information to get out of date. The best option is to make sure your core list is as precise as possible, and pencil in time for updating at least once or twice a year.

KNOW YOUR MEDIA

However limited or extended your media list becomes, a golden rule is to know what each title wants before you start sending material. If you don't know the nature of the media you're targeting you won't be able to send information which they can use, wasting everyone's time and possibly gaining yourself a bad reputation.

This may seem an unmanageable task, especially if your media list is as long as your arm, so start by dividing the list into A and B groups, even C and D if appropriate. The A list will be the most important and these you really have to get to know inside out. You probably already receive regular copies of key magazines, keep an eye on specific websites, or watch or listen to the most relevant programmes, so you'll have a feel for content, balance and style, and can therefore identify the type of opportunities which may be available. You'll also quickly become aware of the approach taken by specific correspondents, and especially of the issues in which they take a particular interest.

The other categories on your list need less intensive research – a quick website visit will tell you some basic facts and figures, and most sites have a specific section for 'media information', aimed primarily at advertisers but useful for PR as well. Some categories also don't need much research if you only ever target them occasionally. The regional daily press, for example, is pretty similar nationwide, but some newspapers may also publish additional supplements or magazines which might be useful to know about, especially if you are planning a consumer campaign.

In reality, it will probably be impossible for you to monitor all the media which could possibly cover your news – if such in depth knowledge really is important, then it might be time to consider hiring a PR firm who can do this on your behalf, or who already have this knowledge from working with other similar clients (for more on this, see page 222). You should, however, at least attempt to gain a working knowledge of the different categories of media you want to target, as this will help you both tailor your information more precisely, and prepare more focused media lists.

Letting the media know about you – what to send where

You've identified your key target media – now you need to decide how best to let them know about your organization and all the interesting things that it does. This can be done in a number of ways (all of which are covered in more detail later in this chapter), including:

▶ *sending unsolicited material, primarily press releases.*
▶ *submitting a contribution to a planned feature.*
▶ *contacting a journalist directly – in order to 'place' editorial, offer an exclusive, to encourage a journalist to follow a story up in more detail, or simply to try and develop an ongoing relationship which could result in material being commissioned.*
▶ *inviting the media to attend or cover a specific event, designed primarily to generate news opportunities – a press launch or other similar occasion.*

Insight
There are many different ways of sending information to the media – by using a variety of methods you can increase your chances of media coverage, and coverage of different aspects of your organization, and start building relationships with key journalists.

PRESS RELEASES AND OTHER FORMS OF UNSOLICITED PRESS MATERIAL

Press releases
A press release is the basic building block of a media liaison campaign, and is likely to be the most common type of press information you'll issue. A regular flow of press releases can start to generate consistent coverage in some of your key media; they are also an invaluable foot in the door. If well written and relevant, a press release alerts the journalist to your presence, prompting further contact and (after your press releases have been used) certainly giving you an excuse to ring directly to see if you can develop the relationship further.

There is an art to writing a good press release. Your aim is to produce a piece of copy which a journalist can reproduce virtually verbatim, and so the better written the release, the better the chance that it will get used. If a journalist can't grasp the story within the first few lines then the release will be binned, so perfecting the technique of writing press releases is essential – and is one of the reasons why so many PR professionals are ex-journalists. This also underlines the importance of knowing your media – if your press release is destined for a specific print publication, for example, and is written in the style of that publication, then it will be even more relevant. As a result, you may have to write a number of versions of a press release if you hope to target disparate press with the same news (which may be the case if, for example, you're launching a product which is equally relevant to two different audiences, such as anything for children and their parents).

The addition of a photograph or illustration can increase the chances of a press release being used – and certainly increase its impact on the page – although this may incur some additional costs; this issue is explored later in this section (see page 51).

What news?
Press releases should only feature news – so what stories merit a press release? Here are some common examples:

▶ *New products or product developments.*
▶ *New services.*
▶ *Major contract announcements (mentioning actual sums involved is also good).*
▶ *Major business developments (i.e. increased profits, new offices).*
▶ *New appointments or promotions.*
▶ *New marketing promotions (i.e. competitions, award ceremonies, brochures, websites).*
▶ *Events (i.e. seminars, conferences, trade shows).*
▶ *Survey results – either from ongoing market research, for example, or specially commissioned for PR.*

As you begin to hold regular PR meetings you can go down a checklist such as this and identify all the likely material that your organization could supply – and it might be more than you think!

It often takes longer than expected to produce press releases, especially if you have to wait for additional information or approval from a third party (such as when announcing a new business deal), so it's often a good idea to have more than one in preparation at any one time, so that you can maintain a regular stream of news.

WRITING A PRESS RELEASE

Once you've decided on subject matter then it's time to draft your release. Unfortunately good writing is a talent which is not easy to teach – and you may find that writing succinctly and legibly are hard skills to master at first, which is why many organizations use professional writers to prepare press information. However, if you take heed of the following guidelines, then your efforts should have a good chance of success:

Layout

▶ *Use double spaced text, and include a reference code repeated on every page, and on any accompanying photographs. Depending on the needs of the target media, you can include a photo within the press release, with a higher resolution sent as a separate file. Date the press release (month and year is usually enough if targeting monthly media). Mark clearly where the copy ends (by typing '-ends-' after the last sentence), and indicate how many pages the press release comprises.*

▶ *At the end of the release, always provide contact details – usually a name, telephone, and email address, followed by the full company address. Usually the contact is the person in charge of PR.*

▶ *Make sure the words 'Press release' or 'Media information' appear clearly on the document so that there is no ambiguity about the nature of the information provided. Many organizations have a specific 'press paper' template designed for use in all PR activities, also making it much clearer to identify which information is destined to be sent to the media.*

▶ *If the press release is part of an email, rather than an attachment, make it clear that the message is a press release, that the release is dated, and that the name of the issuing organization is immediately clear. Content must be presented in short paragraphs, and the journalist must be able to read all the most important points within the opening message screen. This may mean sending out an edited version of a longer release which can then be accessed by a link to your online news room on your website (see page 104 for more detail).*

Embargo dates

Embargo dates are usually reserved for stories which are time critical and which are released simultaneously to a number of different media, so that no one is allowed to cover the information exclusively (whether the journalist respects the embargo is another matter!). They are also used ahead of launch events or exhibitions. If you embargo a press release you need to make this very clear in the headline, and give the exact date (even time) before which the news should not be used.

Content

Any journalist, looking at a press release for the first time, will ask 'so what?' Why should I publish this piece of news rather than any of the other 100 releases I received today? You need to make it crystal clear – from the very first line of copy – why the story is news, and why it's relevant to that journalist and that publication.

- ▶ *Title your release clearly and succinctly – it's important to start getting your message across immediately. Don't be tempted to use a funny headline, unless you can be absolutely sure it will enhance rather than detract from your core message. As well as hiding the nature of the story, it's the sub-editor's job to write headlines and so it's likely that whatever you produce will be changed anyway. A sub-heading, under the main headline, can help provide further detail if you can't fit all the necessary information succinctly into the title.*
- ▶ *Never begin the release by writing 'We are pleased to announce ...' or other such portentous phrase. Remember that you are trying to produce a piece of copy that can be used with the minimum of editorial input – how many newspaper articles do you read that begin 'We are pleased ...'?*

▶ *Summarize the whole story in the first paragraph. Journalists will edit a press release from the bottom up and so if they decide that there's only room for a few lines, these will be lifted straight from the opening section – so it's crucial that these few lines get the full story across.*

▶ *Use the second and third paragraphs to expand upon your theme – providing relevant background and additional information to flesh out the basic story. Quotes can lift a press release, as long as they are concise and help the story along. Using a quote from a satisfied customer, for example, can also provide added endorsement. If you are using quotes then make sure they are approved for use first – the issue of approval is examined later in this chapter.*

▶ *Opinions may vary, but according to this author, the ideal length for a press release is no more than two pages. However, there may well be additional information that could prove useful to a journalist – company facts and figures for example, or more background to a particular technology. Rather than add these to the body of the release, where they may simply dilute the thrust of the main story, include the information as an 'Editor's note' which is placed at the end of the release, literally after the '-ends-' line.*

   Many organizations add a 'boilerplate' to the end of every press release – a standard paragraph describing, for example, the organization and what it does, or the nature of a partnership or collaboration. This may be useful if you are targeting a new audience, but don't make such a paragraph any longer than absolutely necessary, as it is for information only. Boilerplates are useful, however, if you want to make sure that crucial information is reproduced as accurately as possible.

▶ *If you are hoping to attract the attention of a TV or radio journalist then emphasize any visual aspects of the story, or anything that would be of interest to listeners. You can do this both within the 'body copy' and expand this as an 'Editor's note'.*

So many instructions! But in practice, these rules provide an almost foolproof way of ensuring that the end result will do its job effectively. So let's see how they work.

Back at Klipp'ems headquarters, the marketing manager is battling with a press release for the gift trade press, which she knows mainly prints short, snappy pieces covering latest products – here's her first attempt:

Klipp'ems now available for gift shops

Klipp'ems is pleased to announce the availability of its new re-usable staple for sale in gift shops. The staple is set to revolutionize offices around the world, as it provides the first, fully re-usable paper fastening system.

Klipp'ems are available in a range of sizes and colours, and are suitable for any type of paper fastening, from two sheets of paper to documents of up to 500 sheets. This system uses a special, flexible metal clip, attached and removed with a special device. Not only does the Klipp'em hold documents together securely, but it doesn't damage the top and bottom sheets when it is removed.

Klipp'ems will be used in offices and homes – everywhere where anyone needs to keep their papers in order.

For more information, contact Sarah Murray, Marketing Director, tel: 01223 123 456, sarah.murray@klippems.com

Klipp'ems Ltd, Unit 22a, Golding Industrial Estate, Cambridge.

Sarah knows what she wants to say, but is having trouble getting it across. She's also forgotten the needs of her target audience. They need to know not only about the product, but also why they, as gift shop owners, should be selling it.

Let's try and rewrite it for her, remembering the guidelines we established earlier:

PRESS INFORMATION

Ref: KPR1 August 2010

Klipp'ems re-usable staple – gift packs now available

The Klipp'ems re-usable paper fastener, launched successfully earlier this year, is now available in a special gift pack, aimed for home office, student and domestic users. The pack comprises a Klipp'ems device, available in a range of unusual designs and colours, and a supply of Klipp'ems fasteners in three sizes. Additional Klipp'ems are also available in packs raging from 100 to 500, and in a variety of sizes. An ideal present for all ages, the gift packs will be promoted heavily in the consumer press, and will also be supported by a nationwide advertising campaign.

The gift packs can be supplied loose, or in a specially designed counter-top display, and are available in a range of designs.

The Klipp'ems system uses a flexible metal clip to hold up to 500 pages together safely and securely. The clip is attached and removed with a special device and, unlike other similar systems, top and bottom sheets remain intact when the Klipp'em is removed.

-ends-

Editor's note

The Klipp'ems system was invented by company founder Michael Lowe as a by-product of his research into re-usable fixing devices for gardeners and nurserymen. Since its launch in 1999, the system has already won a number of awards for its innovative design, including 'Best new stationery product' from the American Association of Stationery Suppliers.

Press information: Anna Lowe, Press Officer, Tel: 01223 1234569

email: al@klippems.com
www.klippems.com
Klipp'ems Ltd, Unit 22a Golding Industrial Estate, Cambridge

Photograph, ref KPR1, caption: 'The Klipp'ems gift pack is available in a range of designs'

We've now laid the information out properly, clearly detailed the news, summarized the story in the first paragraph and written the whole piece in a style suited to the ideal target publication – a magazine for the gift shop trade – and as I'm sure you'll agree, the end result is already just as you'd expect to read in any trade publication.

Insight

Press releases must be short, concise and in a style suited to the target media – ideally ready for immediate use with no changes. Editors tend to cut press releases from the bottom, so make sure you include all the important information within the first paragraph.

ARTICLES

If you look through any publication, print or online, you'll see a mix of both news stories and longer articles, and many of these articles will have been generated by organizations just like your own, as part of a PR campaign. A longer article obviously brings a range of benefits: more significant exposure in a key media vehicle; a chance to demonstrate knowledge or experience in more detail; a chance to highlight certain individuals and their expertise.

Most articles – especially in the national press – are the result of direct journalist research, but many are originated by a PRO, more so in recent years as magazines are run with less and less staff. Publications often ask organizations directly to produce an article on a specific subject, perhaps following up from a press release;

alternatively they can be 'placed' – the PRO contacts an editor to interest them in a story and then writes it for the magazine. A placed article is exclusive to the publication which prints it, cutting down your total exposure within the marketplace but guaranteeing a greater depth of coverage.

Articles can also be sent unsolicited, but these are often shorter and more general pieces (such as gardening advice for local newspapers, or advice on matters such as tax or law), suitable for wider syndication to a number of likely publications where exclusivity is not expected (for more on syndication, see page 55).

Rather than spend time writing a fully fleshed out article (which can take longer than one thinks), another option is to send a synopsis of the article to an editor, to gauge their opinion. If they want to go ahead, then you can write the article, tailoring it closely to the style of the publication. If not, then you have not wasted any time, and can always send the synopsis on to another magazine.

Articles are expected to be less of a 'puff' – not as overtly promotional as a press release, therefore it's important to get the balance right in the text. You are, of course, allowed to mention your organization, but it may simply be as the company employing the author of the piece (the 'by-line'), or referred to only once or twice throughout the article.

The presentation of an article is the same as for a press release – double-spaced, clearly referenced and with contact names at the end. The length can vary tremendously – an editor will give you a word count, but if preparing an unsolicited submission, then look to see the average length of other articles similar to your own and tailor it to match.

Articles can cover a wide range of subject areas, but broadly speaking they fall into the following categories:

Case histories
An example of how a customer has used your product or service successfully is a very popular way of showcasing the work of your

organization, and demonstrates third-party endorsement. It goes without saying that the more familiar the customer name, the greater the impact of the story, but such stories do have to be handled with care. Your customer must be completely happy about the use of their name within an article which is essentially promoting your organization, and many are wary of giving away information which they may feel to be of benefit to their competitors. But such stories also give your customers free PR, so as a rule they are usually happy to help as long as they are given copy approval before the final draft is dispatched.

Case histories follow a fairly straightforward pattern: what was the problem?; what was the solution?; why was your organization involved?; what benefits did you offer?; why was the end result a success? The aim of the story is to profile the work of your organization, and the more interesting the context the more attractive the story will be to the journalist. A range of good illustrations to support the editorial is essential.

Case histories can take time to produce, but even so extend your schedule when dealing with third parties – gaining agreement to go ahead, conducting the interviews, and then finally gaining their written approval to use the material (see pages 86 and 206 for more on this) can all take longer than expected, especially as you are asking a favour of your client or customer – you can't really chivvy them along if they are dragging their heels. The best you can do is to make them well aware of any deadlines before they agree to contribute, and then hope they abide by these. In addition, be prepared for the whole process to stall, if your customer suddenly has to deal with an emergency for example, or if they decide that press coverage is something they don't want at the moment.

However, as case studies can be used in so many different contexts – websites, hand outs and in presentations – it is worth persisting with them, especially if you are a service organization and keen to generate that all important tangibility. For this reason, many organizations that rely heavily on case studies often prepare them in batches, knowing that some will take longer that others, so that they always have something new to promote.

Discursive articles

If you or your organization has a particular viewpoint about a particular issue or industry trend, then your opinions may prove ideal subject matter for an article, especially if the issue in question is topical or controversial. Discursive articles are often used as a way of promoting a specific person – say a managing director – and as a way of demonstrating the ethos of an organization. Such articles are particularly effective when raising controversial issues, and so you must be sure you can cope with any criticism which may result. Commenting on an industry trend however, perhaps giving your thoughts on what should happen next, can provide a more neutral means of demonstrating industry expertise and knowledge.

Often a head shot of the author of the piece is all that is required by way of illustration – but make sure it is a professional portrait, not a shot from a 'photo-me' booth!

Informative articles

An article which focuses closely upon a specific area of expertise – an aspect of technology for example, a specific skill, a legal issue, or the close examination of a legislative change – can also demonstrate the credentials of an individual, and by inference, the knowledge and experience of an organization as a whole. Once again, topical issues of direct relevance to the reader are often the best source of subject matter, and many editors are glad to be offered ready-made copy on a subject about which they may know very little, but about which they know they should feature something. Diagrams, figures and other supporting illustrations will all be welcomed.

Forthcoming feature diary, and contributions

Most trade publications publish schedules of 'special features' planned for the year ahead, and issue them as part of their 'media pack' – and these can found on most publications' websites, usually published around November of the previous year. Although these planned features are designed primarily as a focus for advertising, relevant editorial contributions are usually welcomed. By maintaining a diary of these forthcoming features, material can be prepared well in advance in order to ensure editorial coverage in the most relevant issue of the magazine's year. If a feature is particularly important, then you could call the features editor ahead of the copy deadline to see exactly what type of material the feature will cover. Often such conversations prompt requests for longer articles, or for material that can be used in later editions of the magazine. Existing press releases, articles and photographs can be built up into a library of approved information that can be dispatched quickly when such opportunities arise.

Syndicated columns

As well as producing in-depth articles, written in response to a specific topic or issue, another idea is to create a 'column' which could be issued regularly. These are often picked up by copy-hungry regional press, especially in regular features such as business pages, but less so by other categories of press, although you could consider negotiating the production of such a column specifically for a key publication if you know that it already carries features of a similar type. Syndicated columns can also be useful if you want to tackle the international press, as it means that the same material can be used again and again, although you will probably need professional help with distribution, scheduling and translation if necessary.

Content could be topical ('What to do in the garden this month') or problem based, providing an answer to a typical scenario ('How to make a will'). Although often used within consumer campaigns, regular advice columns are very popular in business sections – usually the newspaper in question feels honour bound to offer the same opportunity to a number of similar local organizations (lawyers, for example, or accountants) in order to avoid accusations of favouritism, but even so, your name should be one of those regularly occurring if such an opportunity is available.

If you plan a widespread syndication, try to select publications which do not overlap, either in subject matter or the geographical spread of their readership, to allay an editor's fears of repetition and to give limited exclusivity. Send your first column as an introduction, and give the editor an idea of the subjects other

columns could cover, and how often you could provide them
(monthly at most). You can then follow up by phone to identify
those publications happy to use your material, and offering the
column to another publication whenever a first choice refuses.

Insight

If you know you can add to the 'expert comment' so
often found in media reports, then actively promote the
expertise within your organization, in press materials, online,
through social media, or by direct contact. Consider media
training if key expertise lacks confidence when talking to the
media.

'GUIDE TO EXPERTISE': PROMOTING DIRECT ACCESS TO SPECIALISTS

Many journalists cover an increasingly diverse range of stories, but
as they know they cannot be an expert in everything, they rely on
their specialist contacts to supply them with relevant information
as and when required. An online 'guide to expertise' is a useful
means of supplying journalists with a list of such contacts, in the
hope that – if a particular issue comes to the fore – you or your
organization will be contacted to provide expert comment. First
identify the topics on which you would like to be well known,
then put names to these topics – it doesn't matter if the same
name appears more than once. Update the list regularly, as your
knowledge expands, or as new members join your team. Make sure
that the individuals you've listed are happy talking to the press – if
not then you may have to consider finding an alternative, or arrange
for some media training (see page 69 for more information).

Comment

If your organization is closely involved in, is related to, or has a
strong opinion on an issue that is currently in the news, then you may
often feel that you could add to much of the 'expert comment' used
on news programmes and in the press. If so, then scan the national
press daily so that relevant stories can be flagged as they break,
and the journalists who cover them identified. Rather than waiting

to be asked, you can then provide comment on the story either by either emailing a brief statement through to the relevant journalist or newsdesk, or calling the journalist directly – often journalists will be looking for quotes to include as quickly as possible, and if one arrives ready made then they may pick it up and use it. A less immediate response is to draft a letter to the editor, putting your comments into a broader context. Whatever you do, make sure your response reaches the journal in time for the next edition.

Social media can have an important role to play here, as you can make your comments immediately available, in the hope that they may get wider pick up. Gaining that wider pick up may need specialist advice however, so if this is an ongoing part of your campaign, you may want to consult an expert.

ADVERTORIALS

These articles, presented in the style of the publication, are designed to blend in seamlessly with the surrounding copy, although they will have the phrase 'advertisement feature', or something similar, printed on the page. Advertorials can range in extent from a modest half page to a full front-cover wraparound, hiding the real front-cover beneath – whatever the client wants to buy. If written properly and planned well, then an advertorial can be a good method of gaining exposure in a target publication, especially if the timing of such exposure is crucial – a shop opening for example, an appearance at an exhibition, the arrival of a roadshow or a product launch. It can also build a close link with the target audience by appearing to support a favoured publication. Advertorials can also be used to effectively promote a number of different messages at once (if you're launching a product range for example), to explain a complex message in more detail, or if you need to deliver important information which must be reproduced in full.

The greatest advantage of the advertorial is the control it offers over content – although the publication will demand to see and approve the text that is going to be used. It does pay to have the copy written by a professional copywriter – not only will it read more effectively, but a skilful writer will be able to produce an article which blends in with the style of the surrounding pages. Most publications offering advertorials will also offer the services of a journalist who can write the article for you, for a fee.

Although less 'in-your-face' than pure advertising, the advertorial's greatest disadvantage, of course, is that the reader will soon realize that the article is not bona fide editorial, and react accordingly.

COMPETITIONS AND GIVEAWAYS

Most of the giveaways (free samples for the first xx readers to respond) and competitions you see have been devised and then placed by PROs although, just as with advertorials, many magazines increasingly offer structured opportunities for free gifts and other such promotions. Obviously, these activities are well suited to product PR as the product itself can provide the prize, but service organizations can also employ similar strategies, offering their services for free, or simply stumping up a suitable prize and using the competition for pure promotion. In both cases, the coverage given to the competition is valuable, especially if entrants have to visit a website to find out the answer to a question – never mind if anyone enters or not.

Competitions and special offers vary in scope enormously, and you may need to take legal or specialist advice when setting terms and conditions. Some competitions result in sustained coverage over a period of weeks, others appear just on one day. Whatever you decide to do, make sure that you can handle any administration necessary, and establish clearly where responsibilities lie for jobs such as selecting winners and dispatching prizes.

If a competition would suit your target audiences, and would fit in with the aims of your overall campaign, then a good way to decide what to do is to identify what already works well, before devising your own approach. Current favourites include the following:

▶ **Regional and consumer media** *love free gifts, giveaways and simple competitions, and you can syndicate these in the same* way as a column (see above) – but this time demand a positive response from the editor before going ahead. A quick review of your target media will indicate the level at which most competitions are pitched (most are no more than a lucky draw) and prize value can be quite low.

▶ For **trade media**, once again, glance through your key targets to see what is currently being featured. Competitions are common, if the prize is of a reasonable value and relevant to the readership, and these are often run in conjunction with the title. The trade press is more open to the concept of the 'Award', in order to show specific recognition of achievement within an industry (see below).

▶ **National daily media** also feature competitions designed to actively sell publications or to attract readers or listeners, but as exposure will be high so will expected prize value – contact the media you have in mind to establish their minimum prize value before you even begin to consider this as an option. Giveaway slots have become increasingly popular – once again a minimum number of items, or a minimum total product value may be demanded from you and you will have to make sure that you can supply the numbers promised.

AWARD SCHEMES

Although perhaps not strictly speaking purely a media liaison activity (more often coming under the banner of sponsorship), Award schemes are often promoted jointly with relevant media. The benefits are clear – guaranteed exposure and publicity for a sustained period, direct association with a key media vehicle and direct association with a campaign to promote or reward achievement in a specific field. Many Award schemes are set up with the declared intent of becoming an annual event, thus sustaining the sponsors' involvement over an even longer timespan.

Awards can be given to almost anything or anyone, and can be employed within any type of PR programme. Although Award schemes can be sustained for many months, resulting in considerable exposure, prize value may have to be quite high in order to encourage a high number of entrants of sufficient quality.

There is also the added complication of entry administration and judging, and often an event such as a dinner will be required to round off the whole activity, increasing your final budget. However, these added extras can bring all sorts of business networking opportunities, so consider this a key part of the whole exercise.

USING CELEBRITIES

The 'cult' of the celebrity is a phenomenon which has gathered significant pace in recent years, fuelled by simple economics. A newspaper, magazine or other media format will sell more copies, or attract more viewers (and therefore more advertisers) if it features a high profile celebrity and so, not surprisingly, the slimmest of excuses will be found to feature famous faces. Celebrities likewise depend heavily on media interest to sustain their careers, especially insubstantial celebrities whose fame is based perhaps on notoriety, reality TV exposure or on a relationship with someone even more famous. Not surprisingly, PR plays a major role in celebrity promotion, hype and exploitation; any celebrity worth their salt will have their own PRO to manage and control their image for them. Anyone with ambitions of being famous for more than 15 minutes will go directly to a specialist PR adviser for help.

Celebrity is clearly a very powerful force, and one which even the most modest PR campaign can consider exploiting, but not without understanding the implications.

The main reason for using a celebrity is to focus attention immediately on your event, product, charity or issue. As the celebrity is also assumed to endorse whatever they promote, the impact is even greater if the celebrity is 'appropriate' to the activity they are supporting.

So when should you consider adding a celebrity to your list of media 'things to do'? Celebrity endorsement of a 'good cause' is an obvious example of how the relationship can work well for both parties. Many celebrities are already quite open about, say, their political views or the causes they support, so harnessing this is an easy way of gaining instant attention, often with the wholehearted support of the celebrity you've hired (and this may also result, if you are lucky, in a considerable reduction in their fee).

Celebrities also work well when you want some glamour or style added to an event, or to a party or celebration. Not only will they create some good pictures and generate headlines, but they'll also add panache to the invitation and ideally swell the guest list.

Celebrities come in all shapes and sizes – from ageing sports stars to the latest singing sensation, from international names to those known only locally. There are also those people who are very famous, but within a more select orbit. Scientists, entrepreneurs, 'gurus' of all shapes and sizes, even journalists themselves – there's a huge range to choose from so, as always, match your selection to your target audience and the media they follow (if media coverage is part of the plan). Ideally the choice of celebrity should complement the event or activity they are being used to promote – you don't want a celebrity presence that looks too contrived.

Celebrities don't come cheap, and fees for the more famous (and more notorious) can be breathtaking. Celebrities who are well aware that their fame will be short-lived are often anxious to make as much as they can in the time available to them.

Celebrity booking agents are the traditional route to go through in order to discuss terms and prices, but draw up a long list of possibilities before you begin your search. Many celebrities are booked up months ahead (and if they're vital to your campaign you might have to change your schedule to fit theirs) or prove too expensive, or simply won't take your booking.

And remember, there is also a growing market in look-alikes – a cheaper alternative if you're not too serious about making the front page!

CONTACTING JOURNALISTS DIRECTLY

Rather than sending unsolicited material to a journalist, another option is to make direct contact. This may seem like the fastest route to media attention, but even the most seasoned PR professionals only use this technique when they have something concrete to offer – something that they know should be of real interest.

Many PROs bother journalists with irrelevant information, or bother them too often or at the wrong time; as a result, many journalists have developed a love/hate relationship with the PR industry, and can often be quite abrasive when contacted. Simply remember that many journalists cannot survive without input, in some form or other, from PROs and that if you have something valid to offer then the journalist should listen.

Insight

Only call a journalist when you have something constructive to offer – such as an exclusive, informed comment, or ideas for longer articles. Never call to ask why an individual press release wasn't used – press coverage is never guaranteed and you don't want to damage a potentially highly productive relationship.

When to call? In the vast majority of cases, the press material you generate will not merit direct contact, but in the following situations a phone call could be the best course of action:

You want to offer an exclusive

For example, if you have a case study which would be ideal for one of your key target publications, then ring the features editor or relevant correspondent and try to 'place' the article as an exclusive – gaining their agreement to publish the story in a specific issue, and in return guaranteeing that the material will only appear in that publication. The journalist may then decide to write up the story themselves, but it's far more likely that you will have to produce the article by a given deadline, which will at least give you control over content and message.

You want to comment on a current issue

If time is of the essence, then direct contact is the best way to contribute to a story currently in the headlines. If you have a relevant case history for example, or can provide expert comment, then go directly to the journalist covering the story (in whatever media is most appropriate to your campaign) and offer to help in any way you can. Journalists remember contacts who have given them useful material and may return to the same source if a similar situation arises.

You want to develop a relationship with key journalists
The more you issue regular press releases to the core media on your press list, and the more coverage you generate, then the more you'll start to think about 'making contacts'. Although productive relationships can be developed in this way, the value of 'contacts' is often oversold by the PR industry. Journalism is a very mobile profession, and your contacts can move on with remarkable speed. If the quality of your story is good enough, then a journalist will use it whether they've known you for years, or are new in the job. However, as we noted above, from the journalist's point of view, a good contact is worth its weight in gold so if you know you can supply relevant, reliable information on a regular basis, then trying to forge a more direct relationship (especially with more specialist correspondents) is certainly worth attempting.

Once again, you need to find a purpose for making the call – journalists rarely have time to chew the fat – so use excuses such as recent coverage of your news (offer to provide an article expanding on the press release that was used), or call to discuss a forthcoming feature to find out more about editorial opportunities. If relevant to your media campaign, national stringers and freelances (see page 33) are certainly worth getting to know. They are always on the lookout for interesting stories and often work on behalf of more than one publication or programme. If your local community is an important target audience, then try and get to know local journalists – many are well-known figures in their own right, and can be valuable allies in time of crisis.

Whatever you choose to do, however, make sure you angle your story for the readership rather than for the perceived personality of the journalist, as you are then more likely to hit the right note.

If you plan to use direct contact within your media campaign then it's important to understand the way in which a journalist works, if your efforts are to be successful. The following guidelines should prove useful:

▶ *Monthly and weekly publications have set copy deadlines and this information can usually be found on the publication's website. Make sure any contact you make is well before a deadline if your aim is to appear in the next edition. Certainly avoid the period immediately before publication, when the next issue is being 'put to bed', as the journalist will be too busy to pay attention to your call.*

▶ *The best time to contact a journalist working on a national daily newspaper, is between 11 and 12 in the morning. Editorial meetings will be over and there will still be plenty of time to follow up any interesting leads before the next deadline. Between 2 and 3 in the afternoon is another window of opportunity.*

▶ *For journalists working on Sunday papers, Tuesdays or Wednesdays are the best days to get in touch.*

▶ *If your target is a journalist working in the broadcast or online media then it depends upon the nature of their current assignment as to when to make contact: news reporters may be working to hourly deadlines; feature reporters may be working on a series of programmes at a time, and so will be less constrained. The best approach is to make an initial call to find out, if nothing else, the best time to call back!*

▶ *Many – although not all – journalists can be abrupt or even rude when answering unsolicited calls (usually those working in national or larger regional media). As emphasized above, don't call unless you have something relevant to say and have additional material ready to send. Make sure you can answer the most obvious questions – or if you can't, then have someone to hand who can. Get to the point as quickly as possible, allowing the journalist to decide immediately whether or not to continue the conversation.*

▶ *Never ring to ask why a press release wasn't used (unless you've failed to get coverage over a sustained period of* time – *see page xx for more on this). Harassing a journalist will do your relationship with the media no good at all, so instead review the release at your next evaluation meeting, and try to work out why it wasn't printed (see Chapter 11 for more).*

▶ *Visiting key journalists in person can prove a worthwhile exercise. If you are targeting trade press, then you'll soon find that many publications share the same building so you can easily visit a number of journalists in one day. Make firm appointments in advance, rather than turn up unannounced, and don't go empty handed. Take along a few ideas for stories, making sure you have at least one possible exclusive for each publication you visit, and also take along a good range of background information. Look at your Forthcoming Feature Diary for even more ideas. You may end up only spending a few minutes chatting in the reception area, but you will have strengthened a potentially valuable contact, and allowed the journalist to put a face to a name.*

▶ *Always keep a record of any conversation with journalists who call you (and see below for more on how to handle these calls). You need to record who called; when they called; what they wanted; and how you responded. You'll soon build up a database of contacts who have shown positive interest in your organization, and details of the type of story in which they are interested, and this record is also useful when evaluating your PR campaign.*

Insight

Don't panic if a journalist calls you unexpectedly – note down the questions asked and request a few minutes to prepare your answers (but remember to call back if promised). Never say 'no comment' unless there's no other option (you're in the middle of a crisis, for example).

IF A JOURNALIST CALLS YOU

If your media campaign is starting to generate positive interest, then you should find that journalists start to call you – especially if you become well known as a source of expertise (see page 56), or as a 'good example' of a particular industry or trend, or simply a reliable source of well written copy. On the other hand, if you have attracted bad publicity, then journalists may hound you for less positive reasons.

Whatever the circumstances, don't panic if a journalist calls – remember the following golden rules:

▶ *Don't feel obliged to provide off-the-cuff answers if a journalist demands an instant response (usually because they have a pressing deadline). Simply determine the nature of the questions they want to ask and say you'll call back in five minutes with your answers. This allows you to get your thoughts in order, and to consult colleagues if you need additional information. However, don't leave an under-prepared PRO to handle the call for you if you don't want to talk to a journalist. Either brief your PRO properly or hand the call to a colleague who is equally well informed.*

▶ *Never say 'no comment' (unless in very specific circumstances – see page 190) – it implies that you are either hiding facts or are running scared from a situation. Instead, issue a simple holding statement, giving reasons why only limited information is available, and indicating when a fuller statement will be available. This is a much more positive response, and maintains your good reputation. If the issue is controversial then work out your response well in advance (see Chapter 8 for more on this).*

▶ *'Off the record' is another remark to be avoided, unless you know and trust the journalist in question, or can be sure that the information won't cause serious damage if 'inadvertently' used.*

▶ *If you promise to return a journalist's call then do so as quickly as possible. You don't know when their deadline is, and if they can't get a comment from you, then they'll simply call the next contact on their list – probably a rival organization. Make sure procedures are in place to handle*

*journalist calls when you're not available, so that vital
opportunities aren't wasted.*

▶ *If the prospect of talking to a journalist worries you, but you
know that it could become an important part of your job,
then consider media training (see page 56 for more on this).
Often run by current or former journalists, these courses allow
you to develop and practise the skills needed to deal with the
media in a variety of situations, and can prove invaluable in
building confidence.*

How to get on TV and radio

Unless you are a major corporation, with a nationally recognized
name and a PR campaign running 24/7, regular TV and radio
coverage is a bit of a pipe dream. But if you do have a story that
you know would translate into great TV or radio, or are promoting
something highly visual, then you should at least have a go at
getting your name on air.

A few points to remember. Getting regular TV coverage, in
particular, requires a lot of time, energy and tenacity – something
TV companies may have plenty of but which you will have to fit
around your already full working day. It's also a very transient
medium – unless you make a significant impact or are featured
regularly, your presence on screen or air will be brief or quickly
forgotten, unlike a major feature, say, in a monthly publication.
It's also (as is all media) unpredictable – even when your story
has been filmed or recorded there's no guarantee it will be used,
if a more interesting or more urgent story breaks. It could even
be shelved or postponed indefinitely. All these things happen in
print as well, but the time it takes to draft and distribute a press
release is far less than that required to generate broadcast coverage
(especially for TV). In essence, you have to be sure the end result
is worth the effort, and there is no doubt that broadcast coverage
is impressive, can reach a huge, international audience, and can

reinforce coverage already achieved in other media or through other activities. So how can you go about getting some airtime? Here are a few ideas:

Add TV and radio to your distribution list
It may seem obvious, but many PR campaigns focus solely on print and online media and forget about broadcast. If you want TV coverage then programme makers need to know you're out there.

Press releases – stress the visible or audible
Straightforward news – if it's sufficiently important – can get a mention in radio or news bulletins, without the need for accompanying images or interviews. However, if you want to gain more in-depth coverage, then you need to think like a TV or radio producer. Will it make good TV/radio? What can viewers see/hear? Who can I offer for interview? Are they visually presentable? Do they sound good? If the press release provides a package, with all these elements clearly stressed, then the chances of getting noticed increase.

Stock footage
If you want regular coverage, or are already frequently in the news (perhaps you are a major local employer) then you could consider commissioning some professionally shot stock footage, to offer programme makers. This gives the TV producer some ready-to-use images (the reason why a professional is so important) that they can slot into their programme every time your name is mentioned. Such footage usually includes exterior shots of the company HQ, plus some internal shots of people at work, of manufacturing plant or of products in action. The idea is not only to make TV coverage easier, but also to extend the length of the slot you're given, and improve the quality.

Just as with press photography, the footage should be interesting, easy to cut without losing clarity and readily repeatable – and once again, the professional you hire should be able to advise on both what's feasible and what producers want to see. Such footage needs to be kept up to date (so the more general the better in many respects), but this cost can be justified by recycling the footage in other contexts, such as corporate videos or on the website.

Programme ideas

You've probably already seen more than one reality TV programme or documentary about a real life company and thought 'we could have done that'. Well you can try, if you can think of a good enough idea, package it well and follow it up with enthusiasm! If you see a programme which covers a subject or issue you know a lot about, or features an organization similar to your own, then investigate the production company further and see if they accept unsolicited programme ideas. Even if they don't, you could send your details and get on their contact list for future similar projects.

In-house expertise

We looked at the issue of in-house expertise in more detail on page 56, but once again, it's something that should be promoted to radio and TV producers just as to the print and online media. Talking heads, expert comment – these are needed all the time, both by news programmes and in longer and more discursive programmes, and especially by talk radio. Actively promoting the expertise available within your organization could lead to some good contacts. But before you go ahead, make sure you consider ...

Media training

Again, we've looked at media training in other contexts (see pages 56 and 174) and it's vital if you want to actively pursue broadcast opportunities. You and your colleagues must be able to talk coherently and precisely at the drop of a hat, in awkward situations, in front of hot lights and microphones, and give the producers material they want to use – and if you can prove you can do this effectively, without embarrassing your organization or the producer who gave you the opportunity, then the chances are you'll be used again and again. Depending on how serious you are, or how many staff could benefit, you can either go on one of the many regular training courses run by specialist companies around the country, or hire a training company to provide an in-house course. Although the latter is more expensive, it will be tailored to your specific circumstances, and will allow your team to practise using examples from your own collective experience.

> **Insight**
> Media training is essential if you plan to develop an ongoing
> relationship with the media, especially radio or TV. Use
> a specialist agency which can replicate a variety of likely
> scenarios, and can even be briefed to ask 'awkward questions'
> to help you prepare for hostile media contact.

Sponsorship

Of course, you can simply buy yourself some airtime by
sponsoring a programme (very expensive – and really in the
realms of advertising) or perhaps by supplying materials or
products free of charge, with the aim of getting a credit either
directly on the programme, at the end, or in accompanying
programme information (fact sheets for example). Depending on
the relationship you have with the programme, this can also yield
some reciprocal publicity, if you can add an 'As seen on ...' sticker
to the product in question. Again, research programme makers
involved in those areas relevant to you in order to target your
efforts more effectively.

Using specialist help

As in every other area of PR, there are specialists on hand to
help you explore the possibilities of gaining more TV and radio
coverage. It may be worth investing in their expertise if such
coverage could contribute significantly to a campaign, as this type
of knowledge is difficult to build up in house unless you launch
such campaigns on a regular basis. Once again, the media agencies
mentioned in earlier sections often offer TV and radio-based
services, so explore what they can offer.

Press conferences and launches

Inviting the press to witness the unveiling of a new product or to
hear the formal announcement of interesting news can prove highly
effective: it can focus attention clearly on your news, hopefully
gaining consistent, simultaneous coverage across a broad range of

different media; it can provide an opportunity for you to contact and hopefully meet many of the journalists with whom you'd like to do more work in future; and it can provide a good excuse for corporate entertainment – getting satisfied customers together in the same room is always good for business, and if they have a chance to talk to a journalist then even better!

However, press launches can be expensive and time consuming to organize and can produce relatively disappointing results. Journalists' diaries fill up rapidly with very similar invitations, and the decision to attend may only be made a day or two beforehand – as a result, pre-launch planning can be very frustrating as numbers continually fluctuate, and your launch is constantly in competition with other events, and other news, which may be breaking on the same day. If your media list mainly comprises trade press, then it's also worth remembering that trade publications are spread around the country, so finding a venue convenient for all may be difficult.

All in all, unless your news is truly groundbreaking, it's best to view press launches more as an opportunity for corporate hospitality, networking and as a staff 'thank you' than as an exclusive media event – if you broaden the scope of the event in this way, then you've more chance of being successful in at least one of your aims.

PLANNING A PRESS CONFERENCE

Press conferences need meticulous organization: the following checklist will provide a good starting point, but if you are planning to hold such an event it may be worth hiring the services of PR professionals to make sure the end result is as successful as possible, and provide much needed support for your own staff who could easily be overwhelmed by the amount of planning and administration necessary. Consider:

Venue
An interesting venue, relevant to the occasion, can certainly encourage attendance. Many unusual buildings, museums or other public spaces are now available for hire and so it's worth doing

some creative thinking and looking around, rather than hiring a faceless room in a boring hotel. However, whatever the nature of the venue, make sure the space available suits your needs – for example, it's often a good idea to choose a room which can be divided up into a reception area and a 'theatre' area, enabling guests to leave their dirty cups and saucers behind when the presentation begins. Make sure the space will suit the potential size of your audience, that the room is large enough to handle all the expected guests, but not so large as to make them feel uncomfortable.

Also check that the venue has the following:

- ▶ *easy access (or parking);*
- ▶ *if necessary, enough space to allow film crews (or your own video team) to set up their equipment;*
- ▶ *smaller rooms or quiet spaces for private interviews (between press and speakers);*
- ▶ *good availability, preferably from the evening before, so that any stands and displays can be set up well in advance;*
- ▶ *good communication links;*
- ▶ *catering facilities, or permission to serve food and drink.*

Timing
It may seem obvious, but try to pick a time when you can hope to gain as much attention as possible. Don't pick a date when journalists may all be attending a major trade fair in an associated industry; don't pick a day when there is a national 'event' happening (some web research can help here). You can't control every eventuality, of course, and if a major story breaks on the morning of your event, sending all your invited journalists running in the opposite direction, then you will just have to put it down to bad luck.

If you want to achieve coverage in the national press, time the conference for the morning and email the related press release by noon – you can use an agency to help you if your core team is busy handling the event and can't manage media distribution as well. Guests can stay on for as long as they like over lunch, but do not expect many journalists to do so – some will even leave before the presentation finishes, so make sure all press packs are available on arrival, and that interviews can be set up before the event starts. Picking a day early in the week will also enable Sunday journalists to use the story.

Insight

A 'press launch' is more cost-effective if used as a networking and corporate entertainment activity as well as a means of attracting media attention. Many things can stop a journalist attending an event – and they may cover the news without even turning up.

Press invitations

Inviting the press to a launch event requires more than just an invitation – you really need to work hard to persuade a journalist that it's worth the time spent away from a crowded desk. So what should your invitation pack comprise? Here's the belt and braces approach – prepare:

▶ *a* **basic, embargoed press release**, *providing essential information. If the event itself is part of the news – it's an award ceremony for example, or an important announcement will be made by an important person – then include those details in the release. Otherwise, simply focus on the story – the event is just another mechanism for getting the message across to the media. Add a photograph if possible.*

▶ *a* **covering email** *explaining why the journalists should attend, listing points which can't be made in the release: the relevance of the news opportunities, other interesting guests who could be interviewed, or the range of other products or technologies on display – even the venue if you think it might be a draw. Use bullet points, emboldened script and so on, so that a journalist can pick up on key points straight away.*

▶ *an* **event timetable** *listing start times; slots allotted to photography (these could take place just before and after the main event, as well as during); the presentation itself, plus the timing of individual speakers or demonstrations; Q&A and interview opportunities; and when lunch or other refreshments are going to be served.*

- ▶ **directions** *to the venue.*
- ▶ *some form of* **response mechanism** *which also allows the media to note any special arrangements, e.g. for filming, recording radio interviews, photography or for interviews with speakers.*

To catch the eye of jaded journalists, invitations can also be sent by post, often in increasingly bizarre or complex formats, but most journalists will base their acceptance on the quality of the story rather than the package. However, if you plan to issue invitations by post to other guests who are coming, there is no harm in trying to design an eye-catching invitation card or including a small gift relevant to the event – and it is often said that gold edged invitations prompt a better response that those with no edging at all!

Press invitations should be issued at least four weeks in advance of the event itself, but don't be surprised if only a handful of journalists get back to you. As already mentioned, most editorial teams look at their diaries week by week, to assess all opportunities. Following up invitations by phone is usually essential, and should start two weeks before the event. Although this can be arduous and time consuming, many journalists will have lost or forgotten the information, or may have never even received it. You can entrust this 'phone around' to junior members of your marketing team, but make sure you have senior staff on hand to answer any detailed questions.

Radio, TV and online

Online and broadcast media journalists may need special attention during a press launch, and one member of your PR team should be delegated to look after their needs; film and radio crews can often seem very demanding, but as their coverage may be particularly valuable it's important to give them exactly what they need to do their job effectively. These needs will vary but could include (for TV) specific space to set up and film the main event and any social gathering, space and power for lighting, separate rooms or times for interviews, (and for radio) a chance to record – without background clutter – any relevant noises or sounds, and to carry out interviews uninterrupted.

The presentation

Follow the same advice given to anyone preparing for and delivering a presentation – and there are plenty of books on the subject which offer endless information and useful tips. Structure the content of your presentation along the same lines as a press release – start by summarizing the main story, underlining the most important points, and then go into further detail as necessary. If a detailed technical explanation is required, then it may be useful to share the stage with an expert in this particular field as they will be particularly useful during the question and answer sessions.

The whole presentation should last no more than 45 minutes, and time for questions should be ample. You may find, however, that many journalists may want to interview the speaker in private immediately after the event, so make sure this can be handled easily.

Displays and presentations

Use the event as an excuse to promote your organization as much as possible. Make the venue as attractive as possible, with relevant displays, and ample supplies of marketing material, particularly in the reception area, where guests can view it at their leisure.

Press packs

Information packs should be created for the press, and should contain further information on the subject being presented, and general background information on your organization. Press packs should also contain a press release on the event, relevant photographs, and potted biographies of the speakers – don't worry about being too comprehensive, as most journalists will expect to receive the most relevant information electronically ahead of the event or after, and to gain the extra detail they need from the event itself.

Although officially available only on departure, many press contacts will want to receive the information straight away, especially if they have to leave the event before it officially finishes, so make sure press packs are available on arrival.

During the event
A welcome desk should be staffed throughout the event, and should ideally be placed outside the main room, so that late journalists can be welcomed without disturbing proceedings. Name badges must be handed out to guests as they arrive. These can be colour-coded to indicate members of the press, your staff and any other guests you have added to the list. No member of the press should be left alone during the event. They will be expecting to meet as many people as possible to make the time spent worthwhile, so brief staff to make sure that someone is always in attendance.

Post-event
Invited journalists who fail to turn up must be sent a press pack as soon as possible, and any specific press queries which couldn't be handled at the event should be dealt with ideally the same day, or as soon as you get back to your desk.

Web presentations
Many organizations launch products, run presentations, invite journalists and give interviews all without leaving their own building. A sophisticated, media-focused option, the virtual presentation can be a (relatively) low-cost equivalent of the 'live' alternative, and is particularly valuable if you want to present news to a number of international audiences simultaneously, opening up opportunities previously denied to all but the largest organization. Journalists can be 'invited' to the event by email, can log on during the day (and if this is an international launch then the 'day' will be a 24-hour event), can view presentations and web casts, and visit the 'press centre' to pick up press releases and other information. They can even be offered email interviews – either as exclusives or set up as a web chat during the day. Although much less work is involved in an international 'virtual' launch when compared with a physical series of events, nevertheless technically it can be very demanding, and results in a huge amount of effort concentrated into one day. As a result, you need a team of PR and technical professionals on

hand to make sure the day is a success, and so hiring an agency for an event such as this would be a wise investment.

Insight

Good photography is an asset to any media liaison campaign, but use a professional photographer familiar with PR work to ensure the end result is professional and well suited to media use. Captions can be important, so don't neglect them.

Photographs and other illustrations

Photographs play an important role in a media campaign, and you will have noticed that they should be used wherever appropriate – with press releases, with articles and so on. In many cases a good photo will increase the chance of information being used, as the editor will want to use high impact photography wherever possible – you may even be able to suggest a front cover placement if the shot is particularly good. You'll probably already have a library of relevant shots – products, people, buildings and so on – generated for other marketing activities: many of these will be fine for PR, but you must pass a critical eye over them before they are used, as the demands of the media (and different types of media) are different to those of your company brochure. Photographs for media work tend to be clear, straightforward, and demonstrate (if possible) the main messages of the press release. Brochure photography can tend towards the more conceptual, and is often designed to be used within the context of a layout or with other shots, making it less appropriate for media applications.

New photographs are usually commissioned for use with press releases, adding to the newsworthiness of the whole item. Use a photographer experienced in press work (rather than rely on a member of staff who claims to be skilled with a digital camera); you'll find that many also work for local newspapers, and so will know what is needed. Glancing through any of your target media will soon indicate the type of photograph which works well in a specific context, and your photographer will also be able to advise you on how to set up or stage the shot so that it gives the same message as your press release. Try not to produce photographs which are too conventional, and if you need to use a photograph of people – appointments, contracts, visitors or whatever – then try to avoid the usual shots of people shaking hands, or grouped around the desk pointing awkwardly at a piece of paper (or even worse, holding the phone). These really are hackneyed images, and will actively dissuade people from reading further. Instead try to place people against unusual backdrops or in less formal poses.

CAPTIONS

Provide a caption for every photograph or illustration you supply – not just for information, but also as instant text that can be used as a caption on the page. You should of course explain what's in the picture, but you should also tie the caption into the promotional aims of the accompanying article or press release. For example, if you are sending a photo of your latest model of desk lamp, don't just say 'The latest model of desk lamp from Brite Ideas Ltd' – instead, caption it 'The latest desk lamp from Brite Ideas – stylish design at a bargain price'.

Photographs of people should be captioned in a more straightforward way, clearly indicating name and job title, and who is who if there is more than one person.

FORMAT

Check with your key publications as to the minimum specification required, and use this as standard for all your digital shots. Poor quality digital photography is even worse than the traditional alternative – low-resolution photographs cannot be increased to any significant size without some loss of picture quality, and the end result can look very amateurish. However, there may be issues regarding file size when sending as an email, so if the quality of photograph is crucial (if it's to appear on a big spread for example, or is almost more important than the text, as in any really visual campaign) check with your target media. They may prefer to see a low resolution photo for reference, with a better quality sent through on CD.

COPYRIGHT

Legally, the copyright of photographs resides with the photographer; this does not necessarily restrict your use of the images you've commissioned, but it does prevent you from reproducing the original photograph without the photographer's consent. Don't worry unduly about this – simply ask your photographer to explain the implications of copyright with regard to your own PR campaign.

COLOUR SEPARATION CHARGES

Some trade media levy a fee for the reproduction of photographs – usually termed a colour separation charge – and although modern technology should render this fee irrelevant, it is actually a means for these publications to earn extra revenue. There is little you can do to avoid paying them, other than say no and run the risk (unfortunately quite high) that your press release will not be featured – but usually the cost is relatively modest, especially compared to the equivalent coverage bought as an advert. Many organizations see these charges as a necessary evil and attach a budget to each release in order to cover this cost.

'Bad press' – what to do

There may be no such thing as bad publicity, but if you ever experience negative coverage then your reaction may be less sanguine. The risk of bad press goes hand in hand with a proactive media campaign. Many larger organizations, especially those with a well-established public image, garner bad publicity on a regular basis, and although they don't treat it lightly neither do they seek to challenge every instance of misrepresentation. Likewise, if you suddenly receive worrying coverage, then your first reaction should not be to panic or to harangue the journalist responsible, but to carefully assess the situation and take appropriate action – and we'll look at some examples of responses below.

It's important to remember, in this context, that social media has the potential to amplify bad press or critical coverage, extending coverage and doing so with lightning speed. You may need to be prepared for this if social media is to play a role in your PR campaign (and even if not), whilst also remembering that such coverage can dissipate as quickly as it is generated.

A quick point of information: this chapter deals with the 'bad press' that results from an isolated incident or critical response. If the negative coverage is more sustained, and results from a serious incident, then this may soon turn into a crisis – and for more on Crisis Management, see Chapter 8.

In the same way, 'bad press' might result from something that is not even directed at you personally, but nevertheless can have a damaging impact on your business. Often such press is the fall-out of an event with wider implications, the results of a scientific report for example, a shift in public opinion which suddenly gains added impetus, or a heightened awareness of a certain issue (a 'health scare' is a good example). If such publicity is starting to worry you, then it also falls into the category of a crisis – and so, again, see Chapter 8.

Insight

If you've received any sort of unnecessarily critical, misleading or inaccurate coverage then you must act quickly. Before taking any action, first determine where the fault lies then decide how best to repair the damage – whether asking for a retraction or a correction, for example, and backing up your action on your website.

TIME IS OF THE ESSENCE

Whatever happens, if something needs challenging or correcting it is important that you act quickly. Time really is of the essence, especially given the ephemeral nature of most media and the short memory of readers, viewers or listeners. Of course, this short memory can work to your advantage, but if you actively want to correct a wrong then you need to do it as quickly as you can, whilst the original piece is still reasonably fresh. It's also important that senior staff take on as much of the firefighting as possible, hand in hand with the PRO. If specific points are being countered, or arguments developed, then the journalist will want to talk to someone with all the relevant information to hand – not to a PRO who needs to refer to someone else when responding to key questions. Use your PRO to draft responses and guide actions – not to take the flack.

As we mentioned above, the greater your public profile the higher the risk of bad publicity, but no organization should consider itself immune. Here are some of the more common scenarios, and advice on how to react:

Wrong information
If a newspaper prints the wrong dates for a seminar for example, or a trade magazine misprints a crucial detail within a technical specification, then you'll certainly have the right to groan inwardly and take action. Go through the following steps as quickly as you can:

▶ *Check your original press release or article – make sure the mistake is not your fault, or the fault of any third party which helped you prepare the information.*
▶ *If your press information was correct, contact the offending media target immediately and point out the mistake. Ask if a correction can be printed or broadcast as soon and as prominently as possible – ideally on the same page or at the same point in the programme as the erroneous information occurred. Most editors are happy to correct genuine errors, but they cannot give you a guarantee, especially if more important news breaks in the interim and available space is suddenly at a premium.*
▶ *Judge the overall impact of the error and act accordingly. If it appeared in a relatively unimportant publication, then*

*requesting a correction is probably sufficient. If it occurred in
one of your key media, in the piece which you hoped was going
to gain you most publicity then you may need to do more.
Use your website to provide an additional response – overtly
flagging up the mistake if necessary. Brief any staff members
who may start to receive queries from your customers or other
contacts: give them full details of the error, and an approved
response.*

▶ *If the error came from you, then more urgent action will be
needed, depending on the predicted level of impact. To take
the example of the seminar again: if you've mailed the wrong
date to a press list of 50 publications, then you need to email
immediately with the correct information. Prioritize those
contacts with the most pressing deadlines – if you're lucky,
they may not yet have used the wrong information, and you
can also phone to confirm that the correction has got through
and has a chance of being used. Those media with weekly
or monthly deadlines are less urgent, but nevertheless, if the
incorrect detail is potentially damaging, then phone to ensure
that the correction has been received (thereby giving you
another chance to talk to a journalist contact – so every cloud
can have a silver lining!).*

▶ *Mistakes do happen even in the best regulated press office, but
if you ever experience a scare such as this then you certainly
won't want it to happen again. Undergo a post-mortem after
the event to identify what went wrong. If you have kept your
signed and approved drafts, background information and
notes, then you'll quickly be able to identify where the mistake
originated, and how it slipped through the net. Did senior
staff delegate approval to junior PROs due to pressures of
time? Do you need extra approval loops to prevent this from
happening again? The effort needed to rectify even the smallest
mistake will help convince management that PR shouldn't
always be an afterthought or the responsibility of juniors.*

▶ *If the mistake came from a third party – wrong information
from a co-sponsor for example, or a client in a case
study – then you need to let them know what has happened
as soon as possible, and ideally agree to share the burden of*

administering the correction procedure. Once again, a review
of your approvals process may be needed. Did your external
contact fully appreciate the importance of thoroughly checking
the information? Did you accept the word of a junior staff
member when you should have held out for more senior
approval?

Critical coverage

You cannot always guarantee verbatim coverage of your news,
and the more you edge into the limelight the greater the chance of
critical coverage at some point. This is particularly true if you are
supporting or promoting a more controversial argument or cause,
and if you're developing a more active social media campaign. If
such negative coverage appears, then the following actions should
be considered:

▶ *Evaluate the impact of the coverage (see page 221, Chapter 11,*
  for more on how to quantify impact). Can you afford to simply
  let it go or do you want or need to respond?
▶ *If it's defamatory or libellous, you may need to consider*
  taking legal advice.
▶ *If you decide that you are justified in demanding a right of reply,*
  then analyse the coverage in detail, and prepare a response
  based on each point raised, with additional arguments if
  necessary. When you have your counter-argument clear in
  your head, contact the author of the piece (assuming it's a
  staff writer) or the editor and outline your reaction and the
  response you want to give. Don't phone the journalist before
  you have put your thoughts in order. You run the risk of
  being angry and your argument becoming incoherent, and you
  certainly don't want to alienate either the journalists or media
  vehicles which could be valuable allies in the future. If you're
  lucky, you may be invited to submit a response for publication
  or broadcast – but even if this option is denied, you will at
  least have opened up a dialogue with an interested journalist
  which may prove useful later in your campaign.
▶ *If tackling the author of the piece seems over the top, then*
  consider responding via the letters page or to another

feedback mechanism, if one exists. If the criticism extends to other members of your industry then you could encourage organizations similar to your own to write in and give their views – your trade association or local business allies could also help. Certainly avoid getting into an online 'spat' in response to criticism in social media, but take advice on the best action to take, depending on the social media tool being used.

▶ *Once again, after the event, undertake a post-mortem. Why was the coverage negative? Was the criticism justified? If it was, what are you doing about it and can any positive PR be undertaken in response? If the criticism seems unfair, why was it made in the first place? Once again, can any PR be implemented to help promote a more positive view?*

Misleading coverage

If you are the subject of actively misleading press then you may have greater cause for concern, and, once again, could even consider taking legal advice if you think that the coverage will have damaging repercussions. If the coverage is less worrying, then follow the steps outlined above: prepare your counter-argument; contact the author, journalist or editor; try to get your side of the story covered one way or another. Being able to prove that the coverage was misleading gives you more leverage when it comes to gaining a right of reply, so exploit this advantage as much as possible. You may also wish to publish your response on your website, and have it to hand should any client or other contact get in touch.

Sustained poor coverage

If you suddenly become the focus of concentrated, negative media attention, then you need to react more comprehensively. Once again, analysis of legal considerations, relative impact, and the lifetime of the coverage all needs to be made, but if poor press starts to snowball then it can change the climate of opinion about your organization very quickly. If you suspect – or can foresee – that this is starting to happen, then key elements of the crisis management plan need to be put in place. See Chapter 8 for more on this.

Running a media campaign – administration

A successful media campaign depends greatly upon good administration – and the broader the scope and range of your programme of activities, the greater the administrative support you'll need. So it's important that you have resources in place right from the start. Senior management input is essential, to make sure everything continues to run as smoothly and as effectively as possible, with day to day administration usually left to a junior member of the marketing team, providing an excellent insight into what a PR campaign actually comprises, and also providing the basic raw material for your final evaluation. The bigger your organization, the bigger this team will become, as PR can develop into a major marketing activity in its own right, and skimping on resources (especially manpower) is a sure way to compromise success.

Media campaign administration focuses on the following:

MANAGING CONTACT DATABASES AND DISTRIBUTION

The extent of this job depends greatly upon the nature of the campaign you are planning to run. As we mentioned earlier, you may decide that buying contact details as and when you want them, or hiring an agency to manage dispatch is in fact the best way to control your list. If you decide to create a press list on your own, then keeping the information up to date is very important. Whoever is in charge of managing the press list must check it at least once a quarter – although addresses will remain reasonably static, journalists will change. Records need to be kept of what was sent to which publication, which photos were offered and, ideally, what results were achieved.

PROVIDING A FIRST POINT OF CONTACT

You may want to actively name your administration assistant on any press releases or articles, and on your website, as the contact for 'press information' (if they are capable of handling enquiries efficiently). Even though a journalist will want to talk to an expert, it's useful to have someone readily available to manage the initial conversation, liaise with senior colleagues and deal with any immediate requests – for photos or background information for example, or to set up times for interviews.

APPROVAL SYSTEMS

Approval systems need to be put in place and followed to the letter, to make sure that nothing is dispatched to the press accidentally. Signatures must be gained from all relevant personnel before any material can be issued, to make sure it has been read and approved, and these signed copies must be stored carefully.

If you want to mention the name of any third party in any media information, then you need to gain approval first, and get this approval in writing. This process can prove highly time consuming and laborious, but is absolutely vital if you don't want to end up falling foul of your best customer or prize contact. An administration assistant can manage the overall process, but a senior member of the team may have to step in if the material seems to have got stuck in your customer's in-tray.

PHOTO LIBRARY

A photo library is another administrative responsibility but vital in order to manage all the shots you generate for each press release or press campaign. Ideally, every photo should carry a record of when it was taken, when it was issued and to whom (with a link to the relevant distribution list), and where it has been published. Images taken for other marketing activities, such as the website, brochures or events, could also be added to the PR archive, giving a resource with even greater depth, particularly useful for PR activities such as newsletters or feature articles. A regular cull should be undertaken, to make sure that out of date images – especially of products that change incrementally – are not used by mistake.

MONITORING RESPONSE AND EVALUATION

In Chapter 11 we look more closely at the different ways in which a PR campaign can be evaluated, and as you'll see, there are a number of different activities which can be undertaken. However, all evaluation depends upon efficient administration – that press releases have been logged, cuttings have been logged and filed correctly, that all journalist calls have been recorded, that other feedback has been dealt with appropriately. It's also the job of your admin team to turn all this information into a summary of results which can be presented at the regular PR meeting.

TEST YOURSELF

You are a PR consultant fully versed in all the best-known media liaison techniques. What would you advise in the following situations?:

▶ *The MD of a meat packing company wants to state his opinion on recent changes to export law.*

▶ *A marketing department wants to promote the launch of a new model of electric mini bus, ideal for schools or clubs.*

▶ *A newly appointed sales director has just finished recruiting five new members to his team.*

▶ *A major bank has just adopted the Klipp'ems system in all its local branches.*

PR Matrix
Time to add another column, this time entitled 'Media liaison'. Look at your audiences and messages and decide which messages can be best put across by the sort of media liaison activities we have been looking at in this chapter. We'll be adding other activities to this list in due course, so don't worry if you have large gaps at this stage – but you should find that there will be some media work that can be done for every audience on your list.

4

Communicating directly with
a target audience

In this chapter you will learn:
- *what comprises direct communication*
- *when to use direct communication*

In Chapter 3 we looked in some detail at media liaison, which
many people think of as the only type of PR activity. But there will
be many occasions when it is vital that certain messages, or specific
information reaches your target audience intact, and to rely on
media coverage alone simply isn't enough (and in fact, for many
organizations, media coverage is considered a 'nice to have' and
only secondary to other means of communication). There will also
be many situations in which you'll have a chance to meet target
groups face to face and so you need to be prepared to make the
most of such opportunities.

PR can help provide a strategic direction for direct communication,
ensuring target groups receive information in the most appropriate
way, making sure messages remain consistent and that they are
transmitted using a variety of mechanisms in order to ensure
maximum impact.

When to use direct communication

There are a number of situations in which direct communication is the best, and often most effective, option:

WHEN THE TARGET AUDIENCE IS SMALL AND DISCRETE

Often a key target group comprises only a handful of individuals. Possibly they are highly influential – perhaps they perform a specific role within an industry, and your marketing or PR analysis has identified them as being of key importance, not only for the power and influence which they wield, but also for the respect in which their views are held. Such 'key influencers' are always an important audience to target, and although they will (hopefully) take notice of any press coverage you generate, a more direct, precisely targeted approach will also prove worthwhile.

Even if the audience is not so influential, if it is small, easily identified, and its needs are relatively specific (a niche industry sector, for example) then direct contact will certainly be a more efficient way of getting a message across. Use of direct mechanisms enable you to tailor your information to the interests of the group, and so deliver material which is more relevant and of better quality.

WHEN YOU NEED TO COMMUNICATE A HIGHLY PRECISE MESSAGE

You can't rely on the media to transmit your every piece of news and, in many cases, what you consider to be news – although possibly of great interest to your target audience – won't merit media coverage anyway. Diary dates for example for seminars or exhibitions, minor product enhancements, or changes to a sales team – all useful information, but much easier to transmit directly, when you can be sure the information has been received, or is readily available in an easy to access format such as on your website. More important news can also be treated in this fashion – stories such as financial results, important technical changes or organizational restructuring will probably be covered by core media but possibly not in the detail crucial to a full appreciation of the story and its implications. Once again, direct contact – riding on the back of press coverage – can fill in the gaps and ensure complete understanding.

AS A MEANS OF MAKING REGULAR AND CONSISTENT CONTACT

Regular communication is always important – especially if you are marketing a service, and there is no product on the shelf to promote your company for you. Advertising, media coverage, direct mail will all work together to provide a regular shop window for your organization, and regular, direct communication activities will all help to maintain a constant stream of news and information, increasing recognition of your organization even if its services are not being used.

WHEN YOUR AUDIENCE IS DIRECTLY IN FRONT OF YOU!

If you exhibit regularly at trade fairs or exhibitions, present seminars or attend industry conferences, then PR can be used to exploit your physical presence at the event. There are many specific PR opportunities that exhibition organizers provide, and it's important to take advantage of as many of these as possible.

TO IMPROVE THE EFFECTIVENESS OF DISTRIBUTORS OR AGENTS

Although any remote sales force working on your behalf will be managed by your sales team, PR can play an important role in ensuring that strategic and consistent communication is maintained. One of the commonest complaints made by distributors or representatives is that they feel somehow out of the loop when it comes to hearing about developments within your organization. PR can help formalize the mechanisms by which such general information is transmitted to your sales force, wherever they are, helping them to feel more involved and ultimately enabling them to work more effectively on your behalf.

Let's look at some tried and tested ideas for communicating directly with your key target groups:

Newsletters, magazines and ezines

Despite complaints that newsletters – in a variety of formats – seem to proliferate needlessly, every organization still seems to need one. In fact, their very ubiquity can undermine their usefulness, so careful consideration of every aspect of content and production needs to be made to ensure that the end result is worth the effort and cost.

Why produce a newsletter? Well, it's a very good way of gathering together a wide range of information and by doing so demonstrate the full spectrum of activities that your organization undertakes. If you operate across a range of different business areas or have a number of initiatives running concurrently, then you can use the newsletter as a cross-promotional tool. It can highlight activities which customers may not be aware of, underlining the versatility of your organization and possibly encouraging use of, or interest in, other areas of your activity. They are also a good way of keeping people up to date with corporate news – new contracts, new appointments and so on. If your industry is one in which personalities are important (often the case in service industries or consultancies) then newsletters can be used to effectively profile individuals, or show how versatile staff can be – reporting on unusual hobbies or achievements outside work for example. A newsletter is also a very useful piece of 'marketing collateral' (the term used to describe marketing materials in general); it's topical, up to date, easy to read and absorb, and not as 'salesy' as a brochure. This makes the newsletter a very popular handout, and something to put in reception, as it can immediately say a lot about your organization, its people, and what you're up to.

Increasingly, organizations distribute their newsletters as ezines, either as well as a printed version or the only form of newsletter produced. And you can see the reasons why: the elimination of physical print and distribution dramatically reduces both budget and production time, making an ezine a much more flexible option and easy to design and deliver within a relatively short time frame. This has made it much more common within consumer campaigns, allowing even the smallest companies to regularly reach literally millions of people that would be far too difficult and expensive to contact via direct mail. It also provides an easy route directly to your website, and can produce very accurate information on the specific interests of your audiences. However, not everyone welcomes another 'unnecessary' item clogging up their inbox, and whereas a physical newsletter may simply be put to one side to be looked at later, a click of the button can delete the ezine forever (for more on ezines, see page 97). There are many specialist ezine and email marketing organizations who can help you make the most of your budget (for a fee), and may be worth consulting if ezines are to play an important part within your overall campaign, and if you are unsure of the legal or technical implications of anything you are planning.

The best strategy – if a newsletter of some description is essential to your campaign – is probably a combination of the two. The ezine, as well as delivering interesting and ideally valuable content, will also provide your audience with a regular reminder of your presence – perhaps the most valuable function of all. The newsletter will provide a more sustainable and tangible reminder of your presence, and allow you to print longer articles, in a vehicle designed to remain current for a longer period of time.

A bigger, glossier magazine is another option, often produced in tandem with a more regular newsletter, but perhaps only once a year. Magazines represent a significant jump in both budget and production time (and headaches!) and so should only be considered if you think that the end result will really be worth the effort.

So what do you need to consider when planning a newsletter or magazine?:

Frequency

Newsletters are much more effective if they are issued regularly. Frequency depends on a number of factors, but resources and budget will probably be two of the most important, as well as the matter of generating sufficient content. If your plans are fairly modest, then three issues per year is often a good number, to be distributed in September (when people are back at their desks after the summer), January or February (after the Christmas break) and then late spring. Avoid the main summer period, which is often quite a dead time, and make sure your dispatch schedule doesn't run into other major holidays such as Easter.

It's easier to issue an ezine more frequently than a newsletter – costs are lower, and as the extent of an ezine is usually quite limited it doesn't take as long to put together. If you have the time, then a monthly edition works well. It gives the regular reminder you want to provide, without appearing too intrusive.

Magazines are not expected to be delivered with such regularity, unless you are a particularly large organization with a lot of news and views, and where a newsletter may actually appear a little flimsy. Annual publication is often considered sufficient.

Content

When planning the content of your newsletter make sure that you don't just grab thankfully at any available material. Your newsletter will only ever be as good as the material it contains, so try to keep an editorial plan in mind, considering issues such as:

▶ **Who is the newsletter for?** *Back to target audience again. Most organizations produce a single newsletter which is circulated to virtually everyone on their target list, as the news featured is* of general interest to readers of all types. But if your audiences are large, and have a very different range of interests or issues, then more targeted newsletters may be worth considering – a newsletter for customers, for example, would be very different from a staff or distributor newsletter. Once again, the ezine offers a cheaper option for the delivery of targeted information. Keep your target audiences in mind throughout the rest of your planning process.

▶ **How big is the newsletter?** *A fairly basic point, but at the top of your agenda must be an awareness of the amount of space you've got to fill, which will, in turn, be determined by the budget you have allocated. Once your design is in place (see below) you'll have a good idea of the average number of words needed to fill a page (remembering to allow room for headlines and photos). You can then decide the balance of copy on each page (which news will merit a full article, which can be presented as a snippet and so on), and write your text accordingly.*

▶ **Will all sections of your organization get equal coverage?** *Do you need to give each team, division or group a section of their own, or should you devote a special feature per issue to each in turn? Consider your decision in the light of your marketing and PR aims – should you focus on your most profitable divisions or on those which need business most? Which areas of your business can generate the most interesting copy?*

▶ **What news should you include?** *Review what has happened to your organization since the last edition, and identify any press releases which can be recycled, those just about to be sent out, and any stories which have to be written from scratch.*

▶ **How should you balance the copy?** *Decide how you want to divide up the space you've got between news, case histories, opinion articles and so on. What should you put on the front page? Often a template is used so that each page is allocated to a specific business area, activity or division.*

▶ **What regular items do you need to include?** *These could be diary dates, appointments, or business news for example, or even a regular 'thought piece' or profile of a member of* *your team. Again, a template is useful here in helping you make sure all your bases are covered.*

▶ **What will happen during the time this issue is current?** *Will any conferences, product launches or other important events take place? Should you promote anything in advance?*

▶ **Have you included a range of contact details?** *Don't forget your website address, and contact information for any regional offices if relevant. You could also provide a direct link to the authors of specific articles or features, making it even easier for potential new customers to investigate relevant services in more detail.*

▶ *Generating copy can prove to be the hardest part of the whole process, but make sure that your editorial assessment is made on the basis of the needs of your readership, not just on whatever you can scrape together by the deadline! Remember that content can include discursive or opinion pieces as well as straight company or product news – some organizations even pay staff if they submit an article which is worth publishing, so that's also a tactic worth considering. It's a good idea to invite staff to contribute suggestions for content – this encourages a feeling of ownership amongst everyone within your organization, and counteracts any complaints if the next issue does not cover the work of a specific team in any great detail.*

▶ *Don't forget illustrations as well – not all articles will need an accompanying photo or diagram, but you will probably need something on every page to add visual interest. If you don't have anything suitable, you may be able to use a royalty or copyright-free image, or else you can 'hire' images from photo libraries if you have the budget.*

Insight

Printed newsletters – not too promotional, readable and up to date – provide an instant snapshot of your organization, ideal for your reception, as a handout, and something to send contacts on a regular basis. Ezines can be just as useful, but don't use them too often or too freely.

EZINES IN MORE DETAIL

The (relative) ease with which an ezine can be created and dispatched can lead to issues of proliferation which may need to be controlled. You may find that every department within your organization decides an ezine is a good means of communication, possibly even about every product, so some degree of restraint may be necessary to stop your hard work ending up in the junk folder every time. Unless you have material to spare, your ezine will draw heavily on your newsletter or magazine for its content, but it's important not just to regurgitate old news – the ezine has to have some value of its own, and in fact, in future you may decide that the ezine will be the only form of newsletter you publish, so giving it some proper thought now can save time later, and can also enhance the ezine's productivity as a PR tool. When considering copy strategy for your ezine you could:

▶ **Tailor material much more closely to the target audience:** *The ezine gives you the freedom to publish as many versions of your main newsletter as you like – although this will require additional management time and database organisation, the benefits could be great. 'Recasting' content in order to appeal to former customers, for example (while a version to current customers goes out as well), allows you to deliver news in a much more compelling, focused way. Tailored formats also allow the inclusion of smaller news items only of relevance to one target group, which may be dropped from a more general newsletter due to lack of space.*

▶ **Focus on one particular area of interest:** *perhaps extending a story you've covered elsewhere, providing more on a particularly interesting case study, or bringing in some archive material and providing links to related areas on your own or on other websites. Although content will not interest all recipients on your distribution list, it will demonstrate your in-depth knowledge, and give more insight into a particular product range.*

▶ **Focus on highly topical news:** *such as providing comment or feedback on issues in the news (global or from your own industry) that are bubbling up as the ezine is being put together, to give a more personal take on what's going on. On a more prosaic level, you could at the very least provide a more accurate diary of key events (especially those that will take place before your next print newsletter is issued) providing recipients with a reminder of what's coming up.*

Once again, writing copy for a newsletter or ezine is a distinct skill and many organizations hire the services of a professional copywriter to both help them in their editorial decision-making, and to produce copy which is the right length for the space available, which strikes the right note, and which retains a consistency of style throughout the publication.

DESIGN

It's important that a newsletter (and an ezine) has a distinct identity, placing it apart from other forms of literature produced by your organization, and from newsletters produced by others in your field. A title will be needed, and a masthead (the title design, which sits at the top of the front page), and a template design – a standard layout – which can be used for all pages and for all subsequent editions. Make sure the template remains sufficiently flexible so that the end result appears lively and interesting, not too rigid, repetitive, too wordy or too slight, and with plenty of opportunity to include a variety of illustrations.

Unless you have in-house design expertise, the use of a professional designer, experienced in newsletter production, is essential. Despite the availability of customized software, design is a skill which cannot be acquired simply by sitting in front of a screen – and a freely available, commonly used design is just that. You want your newsletter to be a professionally produced document which reflects your corporate identity, and which does not appear to have been put together in the spare bedroom. A designer can also enlist the help of a copywriter, if needed, and oversee print and delivery, although obviously the management time involved in these tasks will add to the cost. You can always ask a designer to create a masthead and template as a one-off job, and then manage subsequent stages in house.

A designer can also help make sure that the newsletter, although having a discrete identity of its own, sits happily with other items of literature you may already produce or have in circulation, and with your website. If you are preparing a bundle of information for a visitor, for example, then the more coherent it all looks when placed together, the more professional the impression. Let your designer see what other items you're already using and make sure their appearance guides subsequent design ideas.

Also, tell the designer how the newsletter is going to be used – if it's primarily for direct mail, then the physical size is important, especially if you want it to fit into a standard envelope. It's important that your ezine also complements corporate design, but it should have a strong identity of its own, to help dispel the impression of recycled news. As with any web-based item, good functionality is expected – it's part of the package in fact – so you need to hire a designer with ezine experience to help you create a document which is both effective and usable. You have to assume that the attention span of the ezine reader is very limited, and that once your message goes off the screen the chances of the ezine being looked at again diminish rapidly over time.

When considering ezine design, keep as much as possible on the 'front page' easily viewed from the browser window, with the focus on key headlines and links allowing the reader to find out more if they want to. Impact is important (within the parameters of your 'corporate' design) as you must work hard to capture the attention of the recipient and make them want to read more.

Creating a template design (just as you would for your print newsletter) also makes things much easier, and allows the ezine editor to handle much of the layout in house.

NEWSLETTER PRINT RUN AND DISTRIBUTION

How many to print? Remember that newsletters have a limited shelf life so don't go overboard – even so it won't take long for you to draw up a fairly sizeable basic mailing list (and once again, make sure you are complying with any database regulations which may apply in your areas of operation). There will be your customers or contacts, then your advisers, suppliers, trade bodies and other such organizations, and you may need extra supplies for exhibition stands, your reception area and other venues which may be happy to hold a supply. You can add selected journalists to your distribution list, if they have already expressed an interest in your organization. Make sure that you can physically cope with the necessary distribution of the newsletter or use a mailing house if the whole process could prove to be too overwhelming.

Newsletters are very easy to print, so don't be afraid of approaching even the smallest local printer for a quote – or your designer can handle this for you. The most important factor, as far as you're concerned, will be the ability to deliver on time.

EZINE DISTRIBUTION

Ideally, you should treat your ezine as a key 'permission marketing' tool – i.e. that it goes only to those who agree to receive it – so you may need to work with your marketing department or web team to work out the best way to gain this permission. In essence, you need to promote subscription as widely as possible – on your website, on your literature, as an 'opt-in' box on any order forms or other response mechanisms. You can drive people to your ezine by offering them 'ezine-only' opportunities (special offers, competitions, giveaways etc.). However, you don't want to send your ezine as unsolicited spam, or fall foul of any laws regarding unsolicited email – and so the best plan is to leave distribution to your IT department, if you have one. If not, it's worth handing over distribution to an external supplier just as you would the major distribution of a newsletter. Managing an email list – adding and deleting names, handling bounced emails, and responding to recipient comment, query or feedback – all this takes time, unless your list is very small and controlled.

FEEDBACK

Once the newsletter has been issued, it would be nice to know how it's been received. Often, the mere fact that you have managed to get something into the in-tray of every member of your target audience is success enough, and as newsletters are not designed as overt selling tools then achieving more than this often really is a bonus. However, if you build in enough opportunities for direct feedback – email addresses for brochures or more information, for example, direct email links to authors of specific articles, or relating to specific features, or links to longer articles published on your website (and we'll look at the use of the web later in this chapter) then you can start to get a feel for how well the newsletter has performed. Don't forget to include straightforward telephone and address details at the end of every newsletter – design a standard box which can simply be dropped into the last page of any design.

Once a year or so, if you think it fits your audience expectations, you could insert a brief questionnaire into the newsletter, inviting general comment and specific feedback, and which could also be used as a means of cleaning your mailing list – you can determine how effective you think this would be, depending on the nature of your target audience. Senior businesspeople, for example, may be very unlikely to respond, but an interest group may be more than willing to tell you what they think, and for these groups, the addition of an incentive (entry into a prize draw, or a pen or voucher for all who respond) can increase response significantly. If you plan to implement a PR audit (see page 23) then obviously use it as a means of determining the usefulness or otherwise of the newsletter, especially when compared to other newsletters your target groups may receive.

Insight

It can take up to two months to produce even a fairly simple newsletter, so don't be too ambitious and plan ahead. Content should represent your whole organization, so don't just use what is easily available – make sure the newsletter reflects your wider marketing or business strategy.

PRODUCTION SCHEDULE

Once you've decided to go ahead with a newsletter, then draw up a production schedule to make sure that every stage is given sufficient time. Work backwards from your ideal delivery date, and always allow extra time at each stage in order to cope with the unexpected. The final schedule will depend greatly on the number of pages you intend to prepare, but the following – for a four-page newsletter, with a print run of 5,000 – will give you some idea of the timescales involved:

Weeks one to two
▶ *Gather together background material for copy and brief team members if extra material is needed or interviews have to be set up*
▶ *Source illustrations*
▶ *Brief the copywriter*
▶ *Write copy*

Week three
▶ *First draft copy returned*
▶ *Circulate for comments and return to copywriter for amendments*

Week four
▶ *Second draft copy returned*
▶ *Circulate for final approval*

Week five
▶ *Approvals returned*
▶ *Pass to designer*

Week six
- ▶ *First design proof returned*
- ▶ *Circulate for approval to marketing team only*

Week seven
- ▶ *Design approved and finished*
- ▶ *Pass to printer*

Week eight
- ▶ *Delivery from printer*
- ▶ *Dispatch to mailing list*

So as you'll gather, it can be a two-month process even for a simple four-page newsletter – although if the source material is complete, and your internal approval loop is limited then you can shave some time off here and there. If much of your material is coming from external sources, or approvals need to be gained from third parties, then you may find the whole process takes longer.

However, once you've been through the cycle one or two times you'll find that the routine becomes more automatic, and you'll also be able to better identify and plan for any 'milestones' – points at which the process goes out of your control.

If you plan to issue a monthly ezine then obviously your timetable will be a contracted version of the print equivalent, but it all depends on how you plan to generate and manage content, as to how the deadlines stack up. For example, if content will, essentially, fall out of the print edition, then the initial stages can run in tandem, with the ezine editor waiting for content to come back, just as the print editor will be doing (and usually these will be the same person, making the process even easier). If you are generating completely new content then more editorial time will be required, and if the ezine is monthly, you'll probably find that production is constantly overlapping as new content is commissioned before the current edition has even been issued. One way of keeping this process under control, especially if you are planning a monthly distribution, is to map out as many editions as you can in advance (a year's worth if possible) so you can get ahead of yourself in defining and commissioning content. The beauty of the ezine is its innate flexibility – content can be added or deleted right up to the last minute, and distribution can be shifted (up to a point) if a sudden hitch or opportunity occurs. With core content pre-defined you'll still have plenty of opportunity to add more topical material as the publication date comes near.

Insight
Your website is a key form of direct communication so make sure you use it, promote it and make it relevant. Within your PR campaign, a key role for the website is as a home for your online press room, providing all the resources a journalist may need about an organization.

The website and social media

Every organization with a public profile (no matter how small) should have a website, and in fact not to have is now considered a significant negative. From the PR perspective, the website has become a vital – sometimes the predominant – communication tool (although it's important to remember that the Internet is not reliable everywhere – more on this at the end of the section). Consistency is key here, as the website is so often the first port of call, it will deliver the first tangible impression of your organization – and as everyone knows, first impressions count. As with any marketing or PR activity, your website must be consistent with other items of marketing collateral currently available, and with the image promoted by your PR campaign.

In addition, more and more organizations are using social media to extend their direct communications activities. We looked at social media in more detail in Chapter 3 (page 36) – but it's worth remembering that it can be a powerful direct communication tool, and will certainly be wrapped up within your website strategy, from a PR and communications viewpoint.

As with all technology, things move fast, so rather than homing in on specifics here, work with your web designers and technical experts to create a visually stunning website that meets your operational objectives. Whatever the technology used, however, content and copy style should remain the preserve of the PR, marketing and sales teams, and especially those responsible for corporate communications. Working together, however, technical, creative, marketing and PR specialists can create websites that deliver real PR value in a number of ways:

A MAJOR CHANNEL FOR 'CORPORATE COMMUNICATION'

Whether customer, client, competitor or just interested, anyone researching any organization usually starts with a visit to the website. In PR terms, the advantages are obvious. An instant medium, a website can be changed, updated and revised immediately, and is therefore usually considered the most accurate source of information (and therefore it is crucial that information is up to date or it can cast doubt on the quality of all other content). It's supremely controllable – it gives the visitor an 'experience' which underlines and reinforces 'corporate' image and values, and protects a brand and all it values. And as a communications tool, it's very cost-effective: although site set-up and maintenance costs will vary, once in place the site can carry as much or as little information as you want, tailored to meet the needs of different audiences, and can be changed at the click of a button – all without incurring any extra print or distribution costs.

As a result, a website soon becomes an essential member of the communications team, providing an ongoing information service 24 hours a day.

'LATEST NEWS'

A 'press office', 'press room', 'press centre' or 'latest news' page within your website is essential, even if you are not planning a high profile PR campaign. The press office is the place to put anything you think might be of use or of interest to a journalist, such as:

- ▶ *most recent press releases, together with a press release archive (possibly searchable if it's of a significant size)*
- ▶ *a standard profile of your organization*
- ▶ *facts and figures, including historical background (if it's interesting)*
- ▶ *recent feature articles and links to case studies*
- ▶ *'in the news' – a summary of recent press clippings (but only the most impressive!)*
- ▶ *links to most recent, and past, editions of newsletters, magazines and ezines*
- ▶ *contact details for press officers*
- ▶ *the guide to expertise (see page 56)*
- ▶ *a calendar of events.*

Regarding contact details, if a dedicated (rather than named) email address is provided, the protocol required when handling any messages must be clear. The aim of the press room is to speed up – not delay – your response to journalists' enquiries.

The press room can also play a crucial role in crisis management – for more on this see Chapter 8.

A GLOBAL PRESENCE

The website gives your organization a global storefront, and if you have an international customer base – or would like to encourage one – then a website offers an unrivalled opportunity to underline and reinforce your global presence. However, if you really want to appeal to international audiences you need to present information in an inclusive manner, increasing your global 'stature' and minimizing any local emphasis. This may mean creating more channels for different parts of the world, or restructuring your press site, in particular, to suppress more parochial news in favour of international news or articles which are relevant to your global marketplace. Local stories can always be included, but perhaps they should no longer be the first thing a visiting journalist reads when they enter the press room.

A 'HOME' FOR SOCIAL MEDIA

If social media is important to you (and see page 36 for its use in PR) then many will first come to your website when looking for links to the many and varied facets of your online presence. It's one of the key means of turning a 'static' site into an interactive, ongoing home for a community based on comment and continuous news. As already noted, with social media being such a rapidly evolving environment, specific advice will soon be out of date, so consult an expert on ways you can use your website within your social media strategy.

PUBLICIZING THE WEBSITE

Given the importance of the website to any PR and marketing strategy, promoting the website should always be a key aim, and in particular, you should make sure you support any SEO (Search Engine Optimization) strategy currently in play. Your aim is to drive your website up the rankings so that any search will find you ideally at the top of the list, or at least on the first page. Your web team can guide you on what will work best, but in PR terms, consider:

▶ *Promoting the web address automatically in any and every PR activity – on every press release, newsletter, advertorial, brochure, event stand and sponsorship activity and more. It could be the only contact address given in many circumstances.*

▶ *Promoting new web-based services or developments by press release to the media targets identified in Chapter 3.*

▶ *Making the website a key part of other PR activities. Competitions, for example, may require entrants to visit the website to find the answer to a question, or to register their entry (also providing the opportunity to add new names to your mailing list). You could also have event registration handled from a website, or links from newsletter articles.*

If you have (or would like to have) a global presence, then over-reliance on your website may be counter-productive, especially if you are targeting markets outside the business community – such as in education, for example. Not everyone has free and easy access to technology, and even if they do, not everyone has a sustained power supply. If the Internet is unreliable then your audiences will still need easy access to more 'traditional' sources of information about your organization. Each of your markets may be at a different stage of development as far as Internet access goes, and it is important to understand this and reflect this in your web and PR strategy.

'Positioning papers' or 'white papers'

If you have strong views about a certain issue, want to become known as a 'leading voice' on a developing trend, or want to present the results of a discussion, say at a seminar, then a 'positioning paper' may well be a good vehicle.

Positioning papers usually adopt a simple format – they are not designed to be glossy brochures, but to be serious and thought-provoking. Quality of subject matter and writing is vital, and larger organizations often commission well-known journalists to prepare the copy, even giving them a by-line which in turn adds extra weight to the whole piece.

Positioning papers are a good way of demonstrating expertise within your organization and of providing target audiences with high-quality information which they themselves may find invaluable when researching a particular issue. Such papers are also useful to send to journalists, to promote your organization's knowledge of a certain area, and hopefully to encourage more direct contact at a later date. High-quality material is also welcomed by journalists as a resource they can draw upon if the subject matter arises again, as part of another story.

Corporate profile

A brief summary of your organization and the way it operates is
a 'must-have'. You may already have a corporate brochure, but
brochures tend to be promotional by definition, aiming to convey
both information and image – they are also expensive to produce and
so circulation will be tightly controlled, and they are also becoming
less common as websites take on the role of corporate information
provider. A corporate profile is a simple statement of fact, produced
in the same way as a press release, and can be used to provide
background information for journalists, or for anyone wanting some
general details presented in a quick and accessible format.

As a comprehensive summary of corporate facts and figures, a
corporate profile should include the following information, all of
which is probably already available in some form or another:

▶ *The official name of your organization, and its relationship*
  with any major groups or other bodies.
▶ *Where it is situated (or where all its offices can be found).*
▶ *The number of employees (approximately – this number is*
  always shifting).
▶ *What it does – a summary of the* raison d'être.
▶ *How long it has been doing it for, plus any other pertinent*
  historical facts which might be of interest.
▶ *Its operational structure, giving names of the most senior*
  executives/managers.
▶ *Any financial information you can give.*

As you begin to draft your own you'll no doubt think of other
information which could be included – that's fine, but the final
piece should be no more than one side of A4, as it should act as an
instant source of information for anyone using it. If you find an
A4 limit too constraining, then provide links to web pages where
some information can be expanded on more fully – this may be
necessary when describing the governance of your organization,
if it's particularly complex or extensive, or the full range of

products and services you provide, or even its history, if it is
particularly long.

Exhibition support

Although the number of exhibitions may have declined in recent
years, every industry probably still has one or two major shows
which feature significantly in their annual calendar – either because
they represent a major buying opportunity, or because they are a
niche event attracting high-quality visitors. There are also many
exhibiting opportunities associated with high-profile conferences,
which offer the chance to promote products or services in the
context of thought leadership.

High-profile events will run a whole PR campaign of their own
and part of this is a menu of opportunities for exhibitors. And just
as well – anyone who has ever had anything to do with a trade
show or exhibition knows just how expensive they can be and how
time-consuming to organize, and so it's important that you milk all
possible publicity opportunities that such an event can generate. PR
is an ideal mechanism for exploiting the high-profile exposure that
an exhibition stand at a major event can bring, and so preparing
a mini-PR campaign well ahead of the exhibition opening day is
a good idea. (Note that exhibitions and conferences are also ideal
opportunities for seminars and for public speaking – these two
activities are given specific coverage later in this chapter.) When
putting your PR plan together, devise a checklist including the
following ideas:

PLANNED OPPORTUNITIES

A range of planned PR opportunities will be offered to exhibitors, from the basic free listings in the show catalogue, to expensive sponsorship opportunities (for more on sponsorship in general, see page 70) – you'll have to judge how much money you want to spend and how much impact you need to make. With specific regard to sponsorship, if you want to take advantage of some of the most high-profile opportunities – sponsoring the whole event, for example, or a keynote address, or an opening night drinks party – you'll have to be quick off the mark. Often they are booked as soon as the previous year's event closes, but many of the smaller opportunities – sponsoring publicity material for example – will remain an option until nearer the opening day. See Chapter 5 for more on how to assess sponsorship options.

PRE-SHOW AND POST-SHOW MEDIA COVERAGE

If the exhibition is a major event, then all the main trade papers will cover it in some depth, and many will run preview features ahead of the opening day. Make sure you know the deadlines for these, and issue a press release announcing your stand number, and the main reasons why delegates should come and visit – issue a photo along with the release if you can. Send an adapted version of the release to all the magazines which only cover the event after it has happened, again with a photo if possible – don't attempt a shot of the stand, unless the stand design is exceptionally arresting. Most stand shots are at best generally illustrative, and it will be hard to identify the products or services that you are really trying to promote.

Check to see if radio or TV will be in attendance at the show and send an adapted release to the relevant stations, making the most of any audio or visual highlights which could attract a journalist to your stand.

PRESS-PACKS

Most exhibitions reserve a special room for the press, or at least an online media centre, and exhibitors may be invited to provide press packs for display, or provide links which will appear on the exhibition website. In theory, only journalists will enter the room and take away relevant information – in practice, press packs can disappear with amazing speed, and one wonders if it's really the press or one's competitors who have benefited from the free supply of information!

Press packs are important, however, and although a limited supply should be available in the press room, it's a better idea to keep some on the stand itself, to hand to any journalist who might be passing or to give to those you've specifically arranged to meet.

A press pack should include some or all of the following:

▶ *a general round-up press release, similar to the pre-show release already issued but obviously in the present tense;*
▶ *individual releases on the specific stories promoted at the show, new products, new services for example, or new technologies;*
▶ *technical data sheets if necessary (single sheets providing technical background information);*
▶ *photographs, as appropriate – these need not be hard copies – you could provide a reference sheet of images which can be downloaded from your website;*
▶ *a company profile;*
▶ *a brief range of relevant company literature, such as the latest newsletter.*

You should provide all of the above on a CD or USB stick.

PRESS PREVIEW EVENTS

Some exhibitions hold press preview evenings, to which the media are invited in order to get their stories in advance, avoiding the crush of the opening day. Make the most of such opportunities – make sure you have plenty of press packs to hand, plenty of refreshments, and that you have enough staff on the stand to be able to provide information and answers. It's no use if all the media visiting your stand have to wait until they can talk to one individual. They will simply lose interest and wander off.

MEDIA INVITATIONS

As well as sending press releases, don't forget to get in touch with key press contacts directly. If there is a press preview event, then make sure they know that you will be taking part or invite them to make an appointment to visit the stand at a time apart from the other media, when they will be able to talk in peace to key individuals. It's worth chasing up such invitations by phone, as journalists will be inundated with similar requests.

ON- AND OFF-STAND PROMOTIONS

An exhibition is a great opportunity to offer corporate hospitality, or to take advantage of any seminar or conference programme that may be running in parallel with the main event. Rooms will often be available in which to host drinks receptions or buffet lunches for key contacts (including press) or you can sponsor a refreshment break for the general delegate crowd. There may also be opportunities to host a seminar or provide a speaker. See Chapter 6 for more on corporate hospitality, and how to make the most of opportunities to entertain, and page 120 for more on seizing public speaking opportunities.

CONTINUING PUBLICITY OPPORTUNITIES

Publicity opportunities will continue even whilst the exhibition is in progress – make sure you know exactly what the organizers have planned so that you take advantage of opportunities, especially if you yourself are having daily 'events' running on your stand.

Tempting though it may be to issue a press release announcing that you had the best show in the history of your organization, it is unlikely to be used. The exhibition will be old news by the time the next issue of your target publication has been put to bed. Instead, this might be a good opportunity to use your ezine, and make sure those targets who you hoped to meet but didn't make it get a copy. It's also something to send to new contacts as soon as possible. It might also be worth mailing press packs to any of the most important contacts who you didn't manage to meet whilst the show was going on, especially if you've just had a launch event as part of the exhibition.

Seminars and roadshows

Seminars and roadshows are a popular PR tool, especially when the messages you want to convey are either quite precise, quite complex or simply informative, and the audience you want to target is well defined, and able to visit a specific venue relatively easily.

For the purposes of this chapter, a seminar is a one-off event, even though it may be repeated or form part of a series, and usually focuses on the expertise of key team members and invited guests. A roadshow is more often the transportation of a more straightforward presentation, exhibition or display to a number of different locations around the country. A seminar can be run on a relatively small budget (compared to the budget for an exhibition, for example) yet can generate significant results. A roadshow is more complex to organize and expensive to stage, but once again the results can be impressive.

Seminars and roadshows can prove highly effective in a number of different ways, providing:

▶ *an opportunity to get in touch with new and existing contacts, raising profile without overtly 'selling' something;*

- *a chance to showcase in-house expertise, and to ally yourself with other relevant bodies or individuals by inviting them to co-host or speak at the event;*
- *a chance to promote your organization to a focused, sympathetic audience;*
- *a good networking opportunity – you will find that many of your guests will often view a seminar or roadshow as an opportunity to network with both your staff and with other business contacts, so making them even better attended;*
- *a chance to mix satisfied clients with potential new clients within the same venue;*
- *a chance to meet contacts face to face, within a positive environment;*
- *an opportunity to generate new business;*
- *regarding roadshows in particular – an opportunity to generate sustained exposure for both your organization and the messages the roadshow (in particular) embodies.*

Insight

A seminar offers a great opportunity for you to showcase your expertise, present your views and ally yourself with key individuals by inviting them onto the panel with you. It's also a good networking opportunity and a chance for corporate hospitality.

PLANNING A SEMINAR

Once again, good, strategic planning is the key to success. The following list provides some basic guidelines:

What to talk about?

Subject matter can be as wide-ranging or as specific as you want – and could be guided by the nature of the audience you hope to attract, or by the strategy of your sales team. General, issue-based seminars are a good idea if you want to use the event as a general awareness-raising exercise by offering your people as a source of free, relatively impartial information and expertise in a particular area (a change in the law, for example, or a new technology). General seminars can appear more impartial, and therefore more authoritative – they can also tackle controversial issues, thus providing more opportunities for press coverage. If speakers include people from outside your organization then even better, as this both dilutes any feelings of 'hard sell', while also linking your organization with experts from other areas.

More specifically targeted seminars, such as those accredited for 'continuing professional development' can also be well attended, but by a highly precise group, and if this serves your purpose better then these will certainly reap higher quality results than events where the audience has a less well-defined profile. Highly specific seminars also serve to showcase your specialist expertise, and raise the reputation of your organization as having the authority to speak on a certain issue. A last point on content – if you only want individuals of a certain level of seniority to attend, then make this clear both in your promotional material but also in the nature of the subject matter, and set the level of debate accordingly.

Encouraging interest

Obviously, the people you invite will know that you are not organizing such an event out of the kindness of your corporate hearts, so you have to make sure you present as impartial an invitation as possible. As noted above, inviting independent speakers to join the presentation panel can prove very effective – or you could even co-host the whole event with a complementary organization. The press, from national dailies to local press, often co-host seminars and other events – after all, they are gaining exposure as well as your organization – and such co-operation can reap a whole range of promotional advantages, as well as guaranteed free publicity for the event itself. The only disadvantage will be the reluctance of other competing media to publicize the event, so if you do decide to approach a media contact with such an idea, make sure that they are the ideal partner and will generate sufficient publicity in order to ensure the event is a success.

Organization

A seminar is a major presentation, and there is a range of books that cover this topic in more detail. See also the section on organizing a press conference for more ideas. However, when running a seminar as part of the PR campaign, the following points need to be considered:

▶ *Make sure the whole event can be fitted comfortably into half a day: give guests refreshments on arrival, present the seminar, and then offer more extensive refreshments afterwards. Remember that for many of your guests, networking is often as important as the event itself, so make sure you create plenty of opportunities for people to circulate and talk, both to each other and to members of your team.*

▶ *Breakfast seminars are a popular choice – starting, say, at 8.30 a.m., they allow delegates to return to their desks by mid-morning, which may make the time spent away from the office easier to justify.*

▶ *Confirm your guest list once your subject matter has been decided: don't forget to include your main business contacts, current and potential clients, suppliers, and the media. If you are inviting outside speakers, or working together with another organization, use this opportunity to exploit their mailing lists in order to make new contacts.*

▶ *The above issues assume your seminar will be invitation only but you could open it up and advertise it more widely, although this will have new implications for possible numbers of attendees, venues and so on. Of course, even if the event is open to all, you can still mail specific invitations to those people who you really want to come.*

▶ *The total number of delegates will depend on the size of the venue – which will in turn depend upon the numbers you hope to invite. If the invitations indicate that places may be limited then responses may be prompt. If response is overwhelming, quickly arrange another seminar to handle the additional interest.*

- ▶ *Email invitations should be clear and informative, and provide an opportunity for those unable to attend to request more information. An email reply mechanism must be included, along with a map of the venue and instructions on how to reach it. As well as detailing the topic of the seminar, and a brief timetable to indicate running order, the invitation should also give more information on those slated to present.*
- ▶ *Issue invitations six to eight weeks ahead of the seminar date. A telechase of key delegates can be instigated if pick up is slow.*
- ▶ *Print your logo, web address, or the name of your organization onto pens or pencils and pads of paper which can be left on the delegates' chairs.*
- ▶ *When selecting a venue choose a central location, easily accessible by road or train, and with ample parking – your office may be good enough. The novelty of the location will be of less importance than the nature of the seminar, but try to find a venue with a good reputation for handling such events as a good venue can positively attract delegates.*
- ▶ *Your guests will be expecting to leave with something, so make sure you prepare at the very least a wallet of information comprising: further information on the topic being discussed (i.e. leaflets, brochures, case histories, technical datasheets); potted biographies of any speakers; background information on your organization, including contact details; information on related topics.*

PR activities to support a seminar

A seminar is 'news' in its own right, and should be promoted as such. If you have decided to run an open seminar then the local press and key trade media will probably be the most relevant to target, so aim to get at least a mention in a diary column, if not in the main editorial. Diary date information can be issued twice – once to make a general announcement, and then again to say that bookings are mounting up. When drafting your press releases, give all the necessary details about the event – date, time, venue and so on, but also stress any interesting or controversial aspects that will attract attention – the subject matter for example, or a well-known speaker.

Post-event publicity should always be considered, especially for invitation-only events, and even more so if a well-known speaker presented. Make sure you take plenty of photos of the event as it progresses, and prepare a press release to announce how successful the seminar was, issuing the release as quickly as possible after the event. If the subject matter was controversial, then that in itself could also become the subject of a press release, especially if a quote could be given as coming from an independent speaker. With the speaker's permission, offer transcripts of the speeches to the media, for use as articles, or in your own positioning papers. You could even offer coverage of the seminar to journalists as an exclusive, if you think that the subject matter and speakers are sufficiently enticing.

ROADSHOWS

A roadshow is the repeated staging of a seminar, presentation, display or exhibition at different venues around the country. Roadshows are ideal if your audiences are geographically widespread, and if direct contact with as many as possible will reap real benefits, which is why they often form part of a consumer campaign, running in conjunction with widespread advertising. Many in the regions are irritated by the constant use of major cities as a focus for promotional events, and so the arrival of a roadshow closer to home may prove surprisingly popular. A media campaign needs be implemented at both national and local levels in order to promote the roadshow and encourage interest – press releases, short syndicated articles, advertorials and promotions such as competitions and giveaways could be organized to coincide with your arrival at a specific venue.

A very wide range of options exists for roadshows, from a simple exhibition stand taken around the reception areas of selected business parks, to a self-contained display, visiting as many venues as possible, through to a high-level seminar, repeated in different venues with different 'visiting' speakers. Given all the possibilities a roadshow represents it's hard to offer general advice – one thing that is common to all multi-site promotions is that they are very hard work, can be expensive, and can also generate a very high level of feedback which you will have to be prepared to deal with whilst the roadshow is running, rather than wait for the roadshow to complete its tour and return to base. You need to be sure the cost and effort will justify the results, and if you are unsure about how to tackle the whole concept, then approach a firm which specializes in such events and will help you both creatively and logistically.

Insight

Public speaking is not just a matter of waiting for an invitation – if it's an activity that would benefit your wider campaign then actively plan to increase speaking opportunities. The key to success, however, is having a good speaker, so consider training if necessary.

Public speaking

How often have you listened to a speaker at an industry event and thought 'I could have done that!' or 'How did they get asked to speak to this audience?' Well, it's not all luck – public speaking opportunities are often a deliberate part of a PR strategy especially if your strategy includes the following aims:

▶ *The need to demonstrate industry knowledge and expertise.*
▶ *The need to exploit and capitalize on the reputation of key individuals.*
▶ *The desire to become a leading 'voice' within an industry or on a certain issue.*

Public speaking opportunities should never be turned down without serious consideration, for they bring a wide range of benefits including:

▶ *The opportunity to address a captive audience on an issue close to your heart.*
▶ *The chance to promote your organization within a 'neutral' environment – you have been invited to speak, rather than explicitly engineering the event yourself and so you will be regarded as an expert, rather than giving a corporate puff.*
▶ *The chance to make a direct impact upon an interested audience, one which may contain a range of new contacts.*
▶ *The opportunity to associate your organization with a particular set of values or issues, and raise its profile within a specific industry.*

But also remember that public speaking has a few very specific drawbacks:

▶ *It promotes the individual, sometimes at the expense of the organization. If you are a service industry for example, and one person gets particularly well known, then they will be the one every client asks for. If public speaking is to become a key activity, then make sure you field a number of different individuals in order to avoid 'personality PR'.*
▶ *Just as a speech can attract a lot of good publicity if everything goes well, it can also prove a disaster if things go badly. Make sure you minimize the risk by preparing as thoroughly as possible for the event, and banning the use of off-the-cuff remarks.*

Public speaking is a skill – you need someone with charisma and confidence to do it well. A poor public speaker can attract negative PR.

So how do you go about generating – and maximizing – public speaking opportunities? Draft an action plan based upon the following:

SUITABLE SUBJECTS

Identify the issues or subjects upon which you and your colleagues want to talk, and about which you feel most knowledgeable – try to identify a mix of the factual, topical and controversial. As we've noted a number of times already, most industries have hot topics of the day and if you can add any new insights or expertise then these could be of great interest to a wider audience. Controversial speeches which challenge accepted wisdom, or cast doubts on an industry development will provide both an enticing item in a conference programme and also good copy for journalists.

SUITABLE EVENTS

Identify all the likely conferences or exhibitions at which you could appear and get details of the conference organizers and any promotional agencies which may be handling programme arrangements. Many conference programmes are finalized months in advance, so make sure you contact the organizers as soon as you possibly can, if only to find out the date by which they need more information on your offer to speak. If you are a delegate at a suitable event, contact the organizers immediately afterwards to get more details about the next opportunity. You may also find that conference companies organize series of events, often on a similar theme, so ask them if they have any other opportunities which you could consider.

GOOD SPEAKERS

Identify all the good speakers within your organization – there is no point fielding anyone who is either too inexperienced or too uncomfortable in such an exposed position. Make sure that even the most experienced presenters receive training at whatever level is appropriate, so that they are ready to present even unexpectedly – a lifesaver if a colleague suddenly has to cancel. Prepare a set of 'potted biographies' for the speakers you have identified, which can be mailed to conference organizers as further information, and which can also be used within programme notes or as handouts.

As you become better known, you'll find that you are asked directly if you can field a speaker – devise a proper response mechanism for such invitations. Before you accept, for example, make sure that the event in question reflects your overall aims, that the audience will include members of your main target groups, and that the surrounding event (if there is one) also provides valuable marketing opportunities. Make sure everyone in your organization knows that invitations to speak should be presented for general discussion – often invitations are the result of personal contact, but the opportunity needs to be evaluated carefully by the wider PR team, and accepted if at all possible.

PR OPPORTUNITIES

Maximize any PR opportunities that speaking may offer: check to see if the organizers are issuing any press releases, and if not, issue one yourself; find out if photos are being taken, and if not, make sure you have a photographer on hand; find out if any media are being invited to the event, and mail them yourself with any additional information (with the organizer's permission); offer your presentation script as a ready-made article to a relevant publication (although, again, check first with the organizer).

Distributor/agent support

If you rely on distributors or agents to sell your products or services for you, then it's important that they remain as well disposed to you as possible, especially if you are only one of a number of organizations which they represent. Although the relationship with distributors will be handled primarily by your sales team, the degree to which this relationship remains successful and productive will depend upon the effectiveness of your communications – So review all such forms of communication with your PR strategy in mind. For example:

IS CONTACT FORMALIZED AND REGULAR?

You probably feel as though you're on the phone to them all the time, but how often is an unsolicited, 'how's it going' call made? Making sure such contact is timetabled as a regular activity can help improve communications greatly – you'll find that you are not constantly having 'problem-centred' conversations, and that both sides may find it more efficient to save up a number of different points to cover in one call rather than deal with each point individually. It will be up to you to decide how often such calls should be made – it can vary from once a week to once a month. The most important thing is that they are done, and a report of the conversation logged.

HOW IS INFORMATION DISSEMINATED?

Ensuring a regular flow of information is important, and the use of email and restricted access websites has greatly increased the speed and ease with which such a flow can be managed and maintained. If your distribution network is extensive enough, then a newsletter (or certainly an ezine) may even be a viable option. Regularity is the key – make sure that whatever you decide to do, it's done regularly, even if it's just to report that there's not much to say!

EARLY WARNING

This can form part of either of the above activities, but it's an important issue to be aware of in its own right. You need to let distributors or agents know in advance of anything which might prove useful and which will help them to do their job more effectively, and especially of anything which may soon become public knowledge. This process is probably automatic when it comes to new products, product improvements or new services, but less so when it comes to marketing initiatives. It is important that they know if and when you are planning to issue a press release, for example, and for them to be aware of the distribution list, or when an article is due to be published in a major trade magazine. Not only will they then be able to gear up for additional customer interest, but they may also be able to capitalize upon it themselves by local promotional activities. They should also be copied in on the circulation of any good media coverage (especially local to their sales area), as they may be able to use the information in their own marketing – as a hand-out for example.

TEMPLATE PACKS

Providing access to online templates for press releases, newsletters or general information sheets for your distributors or agents to use is another tactic to consider, either to be emailed on, or printed out. With the press release template, provide basic layout and content guidelines for a range of standard news releases (such as appointment news, contracts, sales figures etc.). Make it clear that these will be for local issue only so as not to clash with any national initiatives you may be planning. They are a good way of enabling your agents to take advantage of local opportunities for publicity, to which you may not have time or resources to respond, whilst allowing you to remain in control of content and style. Likewise, you can produce newsletters and ezines with spaces for local news so that versions can be produced and issued locally. Give advice on how to best use the material you are providing – many agents or distributors may have little experience of direct publicity, and especially of PR. If you know that some of your representatives are more PR-aware than others, then simply offer this as a service, and invite them to use it if they want to.

EVENTS AND ENTERTAINING

Entertaining always goes down well – your staff finally has a chance to meet and talk to contacts face to face, and your distributors or agents can meet a number of people at once, whilst also enjoying the benefits of your hospitality. The only drawback is the budget, which can mount up alarmingly especially if accommodation and travel costs are taken into account, and can draw the opprobrium of customers, shareholders, advisers and even staff, if budget is perceived as being wasted on a corporate jolly. To make the most of such events, try to tie them into other initiatives – a product launch for example, a trade exhibition, or a technical seminar, and add 'corporate hospitality' as part of the package. Regularity is again important – an annual event held at or near your headquarters is probably the minimum required, with additional events held regionally throughout the year. This is all covered in more detail in Chapter 6.

TEST YOURSELF

▶ *Draft an outline contents list for a four-page, quarterly newsletter for your organization.*

▶ *List your current library of literature – sales, marketing, PR and other – are there any gaps which you can now identify and start to fill?*

▶ *Take just one of your key target audiences – which events would work best for them?*

PR Matrix
Back to that Activity column: would any of the activities we've discussed in this chapter be relevant to your audiences and messages? Add them in!

5

Sponsorship

In this chapter you will learn:
- *why and when to consider sponsorship*
- *about different types of sponsorship*
- *how to evaluate success*

Sponsorship is usually considered to be a more mainstream marketing activity, but it often falls within the PR remit because (a) it represents a form of high-profile, non-overt communication and (b) it usually generates a wide range of PR opportunities in its own right.

For many organizations, sponsorship is potentially a highly successful tool. It can create tangibility, in the form of an event, an occasion or a 'happening'; it can increase awareness among a target audience, maintaining this awareness in a variety of different media, and over a sustained period; and it can generate considerable goodwill for the sponsor from both target audiences and staff, both current and prospective. It can achieve all these things providing the process of sponsorship is managed strategically and evaluated properly.

For many organizations – from charities to schools – commercial sponsorship is no longer the icing on the cake but a crucial part of the mix. As a result sponsorship opportunities are burgeoning as core funding is threatened – in fact, sponsorship is one of the world's fastest growing forms of PR or marketing activity, and so it's not so surprising that sponsorship opportunities sometimes seem endless.

Sponsorship could be defined as the art of corporate giving – in essence you are invited to make a contribution towards the running costs of an activity of some sort, and in return your name will be associated with that activity to a greater or lesser degree (depending upon the amount you pay). Sponsorship can be:

Exclusive
You are the only sponsor, gaining maximum exposure but also bearing all the costs. An exclusive sponsorship is worth considering if the audience is well defined, as there will be minimal wastage from your investment.

Joint
This is usually shared between complementary organizations (perhaps a conference co-sponsored by strategic business allies), or completely unconnected organizations linked only by their support for the organization sponsored, but you can find yourself co-sponsoring with direct competitors – this is usually the case for high-profile events, such as major sporting occasions, where potential sponsors clamour to gain a slice of the sponsorship pie as any exposure is deemed worthwhile.

In kind
A less high-profile, but some would say equally valuable form of sponsorship. Organizations are often invited to lend management or technical expertise to assist in the success of a particular event, or even in the ongoing running of an organization. Such sponsorship is common in the charitable and educational sector, and can prove very valuable to both the organization sponsored and to the staff who become involved in the scheme.

Why sponsor? Pros and cons

Well-organized, accurately targeted sponsorship is a highly effective PR activity as it brings a range of distinct benefits:

RAISED AWARENESS AMONG TARGET AUDIENCES

Sponsorship is not designed to directly generate new sales leads or customers (although associated corporate hospitality may well do so), but it will increase overall awareness of your organization and its 'philosophy', underlined by the nature of the activity benefiting from your support.

DIRECT IDENTIFICATION WITH YOUR TARGET AUDIENCES

This is particularly appropriate when promoting consumer products, but is also relevant to any organization considering a sponsorship opportunity. By sponsoring a certain activity you are saying to your audience, in effect, 'we like what you like' and are therefore attempting to create a 'bond', creating and enhancing the chemistry that is an essential part of the successful relationship with a target group. Remember that this works two ways – some audiences may positively dislike the object of your sponsorship (or at least have no reaction to it either way), so be prepared to either live with this, or to expand your programme to embrace a range of different sponsorships in order to appeal directly to different target groups.

LONG-TERM, HIGH-QUALITY EXPOSURE

Sponsored activities which run for a sustained period of time (such as a competition with a number of stages, or initiatives lasting several months) obviously offer extended benefits, but even one-off events offer a wealth of opportunities before and after the event has taken place. Sustained exposure is particularly useful for service organizations which need to continuously remind the market of their presence. If you don't want to embark upon a prolonged campaign, or haven't the resources to support it properly, then a viable alternative is to sponsor an annual event, such as an award, a concert or competition, with which your name can become synonymous, enabling the sponsorship to work on your behalf even when promotional activities are not taking place.

CREATING CLOSER LINKS BETWEEN YOUR ORGANIZATION AND A 'STRATEGIC ALLY'

Joint sponsorship in particular reaps this specific benefit. We've already considered the idea of co-sponsoring a seminar with a key trade magazine – this is an ideal example of how joint sponsorship can reap even greater benefits than straightforward association. In fact, many sponsorships result from a deliberate aim of forging stronger links with a particular organization. Unexpected synergies can often result from co-sponsoring arrangements – especially if you are unfamiliar with your partners. You may even get some extra business yourself!

IMPROVED IMAGE

Sponsoring a 'good cause' whether charitable, educational or artistic can serve to raise awareness of your organization's philanthropic approach, and civic responsibility. Knock-on effects can include goodwill from customers and staff, stronger ties with the local community – important if its support may be needed in the future – and increased respect among your peers. Association with a good cause can also add an element of 'character' to a possibly faceless organization, and may well provide a number of opportunities for employees to get involved in (or at least learn about) something beyond the scope of their everyday work.

STAFF INVOLVEMENT AND SUPPORT

Sponsorship can be used as an informal element of staff development programmes, helping to develop skills such as team building, planning and project management if staff are also involved in helping develop the sponsorship programme. Staff can also benefit directly from sponsorship, through free tickets to an event for example, and the association of one's employer with a high profile occasion can also help boost morale. Staff can even help direct the sponsorship programme, by highlighting opportunities or by voicing support for a specific cause. You may even find that some of your own staff – particularly amateur sports people – are an ideal vehicle for sponsorship, or that you can encourage staff to come forward with sponsorship requests or ideas, especially for causes close to their heart.

But despite this impressive range of benefits, there are some significant disadvantages which must also be considered:

EXPENSE

You get what you pay for – guaranteed high exposure can translate into high cost. An alternative, although riskier approach is to sponsor a less well-known event and then use PR to promote it to the hilt. Also, your initial budget may easily double by the end of the programme, if you add in your own promotional costs to cover activities such as a dedicated media relations campaign, advertising, corporate hospitality, direct mail, staff time and so on. Sponsorship alone will usually not make sufficient impact without additional marketing support.

SCATTER-GUN MARKETING

Although audience reach may be wide, the net effect of sponsorship can still be hard to isolate. For example, high-profile sports sponsorship may be appealing in terms of the TV exposure gained, but what percentage of the audience is actually influenced by what is, in effect, covert TV advertising? A low key, but more highly focused event – perhaps a charity cricket match to which a large number of targets can be directly invited – may yield more tangible results.

HIGH-PROFILE SUCCESS – HIGH-PROFILE DISASTER

If your sponsorship is based on the supply of any sort of technology or service then it is essential that you perform as demanded or else you will become the focus of bad publicity and serious discontent. Likewise, if the event itself draws negative publicity – for whatever reason – then you may suddenly find yourself associated with a disaster rather than a success, and for no fault of your own. Although more expensive or more controversial sponsorship opportunities may generate more publicity, tight management and control will be essential. A crisis management programme (see Chapter 8), established in advance, can prepare for possible damage limitation should things start to go wrong.

OVERKILL

Increased competition among sponsors for highly popular, well-publicized events, has resulted in a greater division of opportunities as organizers, not surprisingly, aim to generate as much income as possible. The resulting proliferation of sponsors can cause media 'clutter' and confusion among target audiences, with only the top-spending sponsors rising above the noise. It can also result in such a small slice of the cake being available that the end result is negligible.

CYNICISM

The general public rarely views a sponsorship deal as the result of pure corporate philanthropy. It understands that sponsorship happens (even the most altruistic) also because (a) you had the money to spare, (b) you can see some benefit to be gained for your organization and (c) it meets the aims of your PR strategy. But if handled well, the end result need not appear too calculated, and the strong relationship between the sponsor and your organization can build into something that can remain positively beneficial for many years to come. The general public is also well aware that without sponsorship, many popular events would never happen, so they take a realistic approach to the bargain, as long as the sponsor is not seen as taking advantage of the occasion.

Insight

Sponsorship can be an ideal way to gain extended publicity, while also supporting a cause which really needs your help, or which is popular among your target audiences. Be aware of the pros and cons when choosing who or what to sponsor, however.

Developing a sponsorship programme

For most smaller organizations, sponsorship will probably so
far have been a haphazard and opportunistic activity, perhaps
only taking place at trade fairs, or focusing on local events which
provide an opportunity for 'corporate hospitality'. If you want
to think more seriously about sponsorship, then first outline the
criteria to use when evaluating any future opportunities or when
generating your own ideas. Consider:

▶ *Your current marketing and PR strategy and aims and
  objectives, especially key audiences and messages.*
▶ *The broader areas of sponsorship that are most appropriate to
  both your corporate culture and that of your target audiences
  (see below for more on this), and whether you want to sponsor
  some already existing initiative, or devise something of your
  own.*
▶ *The budget you want to allocate.*
▶ *The activities of your competitors – can you compete
  effectively, is the field still wide open, or have certain
  opportunities already become firmly associated with another
  sponsor?*
▶ *How you plan to evaluate the success of the sponsorship, once
  in place (and we'll look at that in more detail at the end of this
  chapter).*

Once you've outlined a broad brief, then you can start to consider
the options open to you. Sometimes it may seem that almost
anything that moves can be sponsored, and in the case of leading
sports personalities, sponsored many times simultaneously. Ideas
for sponsorship vehicles are often 'packaged' and presented to
potential sponsors, but you can also think of ideas of your own,
especially if you have a highly specific aim in mind. In addition,
there are many professional sponsorship consultancies who can
advise on what to do, if you plan to consider sponsorship even
more seriously.

When deciding what to sponsor, revisit your PR aims and objectives, and review your target audiences. Make sure the object of your sponsorship satisfies key criteria, such as an improved direct relationship with key audience groups, empathy with your marketing aims, or strong support from staff.

To start you off, however, let's quickly run through a few of the most popular sponsorship categories:

SPORT

Sponsorship has become an established part of the sporting world, and opportunities range from your local school's sports day to the World Cup.

Advantages
Sports sponsorship has a long history and is therefore an established, safe and relatively straightforward option with local, national and international opportunties. Many major sporting events or organizations offer sponsorship opportunities, and have extensive experience in managing sponsors, their money and their expectations. Teams also need sponsoring, meaning that your name can travel far and wide, especially if the team is successful. Depending upon the chosen sport, sponsorship can also offer good opportunities for corporate hospitality at a generally pleasant, informal occasion. It can also generate very high-profile publicity – particularly in the broadcast media – and is often associated with business values such as competitiveness, endeavour and success. Sports sponsorship is often popular with staff, especially if they can take advantage of free tickets.

Disadvantages
A very wide variety of opportunities exist, but finding an exclusive deal is becoming both more difficult and more expensive. The cost of sponsoring even a small part of a high-profile sporting occasion can also be high, and yet you will still only gain minimal exposure.

The more traditional the sport, the more conservative the end result, and although this may suit certain target groups it may not provide any great differentiation for the sponsor, unless the sponsorship is particularly impressive or generous. In terms of corporate hospitality, there is also the risk that your guests may be jaded by the frequency of such events and therefore be less impressed by an invitation. There has also been a growing resentment among 'fans' attending sporting events that sponsorship clients get all the best seats, used by people not always that interested in what they've come to see. It should also be remembered that different sports appeal to different audiences, so be careful not to make your choice of sponsored sport unintentionally exclusive.

ARTS

Arts sponsorship has become increasingly high profile in recent years, and as a result increasingly well organized.

Advantages
Arts sponsorship can be as conservative or as radical as the sponsor desires, and is associated with imaginative and creative skills, as well as demonstrating taste and education. Many artistic events last over a period of time – an exhibition for example, or a programme of concerts – resulting in longer term exposure and a string of associated opportunities (such as in-gallery entertaining) and long-term publicity. The philanthropic nature of arts sponsorship often reflects favourably upon an organization and it can often prove to be a less expensive option, and one that appeals to a very wide spectrum of people.

Disadvantages
The arts can be seen as elitist, and the events sponsored are often relatively low key. Resulting publicity may be less, and may only be gained in certain media. Many smaller artistic organizations are not as commercially aware as their sporting counterparts,

and therefore more management time from the sponsor may be required to ensure the desired results are achieved.

BUSINESS-TO-BUSINESS

Opportunities are always available to sponsor Awards, events or competitions within the business community, either within your own industry or in 'vertical' markets – markets complementary to your own.

Advantages

High-profile publicity can be generated directly amongst a key target audience without much wastage. Business sponsorships are often joint affairs, allowing the sponsor to get closer to an organization which could be of use in the future – a trade association, for example, or again a key publication. Many sponsorship opportunities centre upon an annual event (in the case of an award, for example), and so the chances for repeat sponsorship are increased, with a greater degree of recognition being achieved each time the cycle starts again, and usually the option of first refusal when sponsorship is up for renewal. Business to business sponsorships tie your organization closely to a particular sector or regional community, and can also demonstrate active support for higher standards, or values such as excellence, performance and ambition.

Disadvantages

Once again, this is a very overcrowded area, and one in which many sponsorships are merely PR exercises, dreamt up to generate extra publicity – as a result they can appear contrived. Care is needed to ensure the sponsorship is worthwhile, and attracts the desired attention. For example, award programmes can backfire if no one enters, or if entries are of the wrong quality. They also demand extra management time in terms of administration and judging of entries (although co-operating with a partner organization, and meeting the judges, offers further opportunities to influence target audiences).

EDUCATION

Sponsorship opportunities are available at all levels of the education system, from nursery school to postgraduate, and are increasing year by year.

Advantages

Fostering direct links with the education system can deliver a number of advantages: improved links with the local community; improved recruitment; the opportunity to raise awareness among students of your products or services – and among parents as well. As schools and colleges clamour for better resources, the opportunities for sponsors to provide these resources are enormous, and many companies exist specifically to help organizations make the most of the education sector, providing guidance on how to link any activities directly to standards of educational achievement, or to meet specific classroom needs.

Disadvantages

Commercial sponsorship in the school system sometimes receives a lukewarm reception: although accepted as unavoidable, it is often criticized as disguised advertising and manipulation of a naive audience. If you attract negative publicity for any other aspect of your business this can also backfire on any educational sponsorships you may be supporting. Involvement at the higher education level can be expensive and – as is the case in any training investment – is no guarantee that the skills or knowledge you aim to encourage will be used on behalf of the sponsoring organization. It is another very crowded market place, and so needs care and good management in order to achieve differentiation.

CHARITABLE OR CAUSE-RELATED SPONSORSHIP

Although many of the sponsorship recipients already considered – arts groups, sports clubs and so on – are already registered as charities, this section refers more to the 'good cause'. Corporate charitable giving has declined in recent years, as the evaluation of return has proved increasingly difficult to assess, and budgets come under closer scrutiny. Charities are well aware of this and have responded by increasing the range and sophistication of the opportunities available, enabling them to compete more effectively with more commercial organizations also battling for a share of the sponsorship pot.

Advantages

Depending on the nature of the charity, sponsorship can generate considerable publicity and goodwill, as well as providing an opportunity for staff involvement at all levels. A long-term relationship, leading to long-term exposure, is positively welcomed, and an organization can become closely associated with a good cause. It's also a good way of fostering closer links with a local community, if the direct benefits of the sponsorship (a mini-bus for example, or a community resource) can be easily appreciated. The choice of a 'good cause' which reflects the nature of an organization can also prove highly valuable – a major employer of female staff could choose to support a breast cancer charity, for example, or a manufacturer of optical products could support a charity working with the partially sighted.

Disadvantages

Opportunities in this area are legion – considerable care is needed when selecting a charity to support, and unless a considerable sum is donated in one direction, very little impact may be made. Sponsorship money may have to be regarded as pump-priming, and additional effort required in order to effect a more tangible and successful end result. Smaller, less well resourced charities will also need greater management input from the sponsor in order to ensure the smooth running of the relationship. Ending a sponsorship agreement can result in negative publicity unless managed carefully.

Insight

For sponsorship to generate worthwhile benefits (for all concerned) it needs to be managed effectively, which can

(Contd)

place extra demands on staff time. Evaluation criteria must also be established at the outset so that success can be measured realistically.

Managing the relationship

Sponsorship is not simply an act of handing over money – it needs to be managed effectively right from the start, beginning with a clear understanding of the expectations of both sides. Ensure that those members of your team who will be running the sponsorship are involved right from the beginning, in order to make sure everyone knows what is expected of them. The amount of management time you or your colleagues will need to donate must also be clearly laid down.

As was said earlier, many organizations are becoming increasingly sophisticated in the way they package their sponsorship opportunities, but even clear cut sponsorship agreements must be well defined in advance in order to avoid arguments down the line. For example, if your logo is to appear whenever a certain event is publicized, then make sure you know exactly how big the logo will be and how it will be used – in a muddle with everyone else's, or clearly on its own? If part of the deal promises corporate hospitality, check on how exclusive this will be – will you be able to entertain clients in your own room or marquee or will you simply be given a supply of free tickets? It's difficult to generalize, because every agreement is different, but it's important to iron out any ambiguities right from the start.

Once the sponsorship is up and running, maintaining contact is vital, and so regular meetings must be part of the agreement. You need to make sure that promised publicity has been organized, you'll want to check the use of your name in any promotional literature or press releases, and you'll want to get a feel for how successful the sponsorship is as soon as it starts to go 'live' – not least to help you plan and implement your own supporting PR campaigns, and publish updates on the sponsorship in your newsletters or on your website.

Evaluation

Sponsorship – as for any broad-based marketing activity – is difficult to evaluate, but evaluation is nevertheless essential in order to ensure spend is maximized, and to establish whether the exercise is worth repeating, especially as many sponsorship deals can last for a considerable amount of time – even years. The key to proper evaluation is the setting of realistic, measurable aims and objectives at the outset of the sponsorship agreement. Here are some examples of how to assess a range of different sponsorship aims:

Aim: increased awareness of your organization's name among key target groups

Look at the concrete achievements, and the nature of the activities undertaken and assess their benefits: assess the frequency of any media coverage for example, and where it was gained and use your own best judgement to evaluate whether it really was working as hard as it could. If your exposure was only limited to a few posters placed in less than successful sites then you may have a right to question the impact your spend has achieved.

Aim: increased coverage in key media

In Chapter 11 we look in more detail at the ways of assessing media coverage, and you can apply these methods to your sponsorship campaign, gaining a feel not only for how often your name was associated with the sponsorship, but also coverage of the sponsorship itself without your name being mentioned – this may give cause for concern, if you discover that your involvement was largely ignored, and you'll want to know why this has happened.

Aim: to increase links with the local community

This is harder to assess, and will depend upon a combination of factors including local press coverage, local exposure in other ways, and the success or otherwise of the event which you were sponsoring. Have you found a greater awareness among current staff or new recruits of your 'presence' in the community? Have you received more direct approaches from other relevant local groups? Who sees your sponsorship as a positive contribution to local life?

See Chapter 11 for more on all the different evaluation techniques that can be applied, and use them in this context.

TEST YOURSELF

Once again, donning your PR consultant's hat, what type of sponsorships would you recommend for the following clients?:

▶ *A high street bank, with a traditional reputation, wanting to raise its profile within the local business community.*

▶ *An online bank with a reputation for modern ideas and new thinking, wanting to raise its profile within the hi-tech community nationwide.*

▶ *The Clean Sweeps – wanting to raise its general profile among prospective clients and add it to your list.*

PR Matrix
Back to your Activity column – could sponsorship provide some good results with your target audiences? See where it could be used and jot it down.

6

Entertaining and corporate hospitality

In this chapter you will learn:
- *when to 'entertain'*
- *what you can do on different budgets*
- *how to make an event a success*

Many people think of PR as a combination of press work and cocktail parties but as I hope we have already demonstrated, nothing could be further from the truth. However, it has to be said that 'corporate entertainment' does usually fall under the remit of the PR department and it can form a very useful – and often very enjoyable – aspect of a PR campaign. Corporate entertaining can extend from a quick lunch down the pub, to a full weekend away for clients and their families, and from a small group event to an 'open house' party – with associated budgetary implications. And remember, entertaining should not just be aimed at your customers and contacts. Your staff and suppliers may also need rewarding, or given a chance to socialize informally. As ever, it's always better to plan strategically, and this goes for entertaining as much as for any other PR activity, even though the end result may be designed to appear spontaneous and unforced.

Before we start, however, let's look at the benefits of corporate entertaining in order to identify those which best suit your PR programme:

An opportunity to develop relationships

Any form of corporate entertaining aims to create an informal
atmosphere in which you can get to know your guests
better – whether they are important prospective clients or long-
serving staff. This is especially valuable to service organizations,
which place a high value on the 'chemistry' that often persuades
a client to use one organization rather than another. Away from
a 'hard-sell' environment, conversation can focus on topics
other than business (and in fact business talk is often actively
discouraged) and a convivial atmosphere, helped along by an
attractive setting or interesting event, can help key relationships
develop at a more fundamental level, paving the way for a stronger
relationship in the future.

An opportunity to target a wide range of audiences

Other events organized as part of your PR programme have
probably focused more closely on specific target audiences.
Entertaining, without the work-related remit, can be used as an
excuse to invite everyone on your target list, and get them together
at the same time. The positive PR that can be generated by a mix
of satisfied and potential customers is tremendous. And the mix of
less obviously related groups – suppliers, for example, and support
staff – can also lead to a much more interesting and fruitful end
result.

As a way of saying 'thank you'

If your organization has been growing rapidly, then it's probably
taken all your time and effort to keep on top of day-to-day
developments. Corporate entertaining gives you the chance to stop
and say 'thank you' to all the people who have helped you so
far – once again, to customers, suppliers, staff – in fact to anyone
who has supported your organization in the past and who you
want to continue doing so in the future. It's also a chance to say
thank you to all those contacts who have invited you to parties
or events in the past, returning their hospitality and further
strengthening relationships.

A night to remember!

The business community, especially a local business community, often views corporate hospitality as an important networking opportunity. As a result, however, such events can occur with increasing frequency and you may find you have to work harder to stand out from the crowd, especially if you want your event to be an occasion to remember and the quality of the guest list to remain high. You yourself may already have been invited to a range of different parties and events – which invitations did you accept and why? Why did you turn down others? Use your own experience to guide your initial thoughts when planning an event of your own, as it's likely that others invited to the same events represent at least some of your key target groups.

If you've decided that entertaining should become part of your PR plan then, once again, outline a strategy which will make the most of your budget. Use the following parameters to help you:

WHO *DO YOU WANT TO 'ENTERTAIN'*?

Make a wish list of all those who you think it would be beneficial to entertain: the list will probably include your most important clients and customers (former, current and potential), key contacts, major suppliers and distributors and, of course, your staff. Don't forget to include those 'key influencers', however, those who are vital to the running of your organization and who may also be able to recommend you to other potential contacts. Include your business advisers, your bank manager, your accountant and others such as management consultants, independent advisers and journalists. The list may now look rather frightening, but it's important to assess the range and scope of contacts you want to entertain – in fact, it may become clear at this stage that you need to consider a number of different options (especially if your ideal guest list is geographically widespread), rather than hold one big bash.

Of course, you can always entertain contacts on a one-to-one basis, but also look at ways in which you can band them together. If you think it's worth hosting an annual 'event' (and we'll look at the sort of thing you could do later in this chapter) then this would be an ideal way of entertaining all your 'A-list' contacts at once. As the cost of such events can prove quite high, you may not think it worth inviting your 'B-list' along, but instead make sure they are invited to events such as seminars, conferences or exhibitions, where hospitality is part of the occasion – once again, this will also enable you to entertain effectively around the country. You may also consider a less expensive option, such as a drinks party, as a better way to entertain such 'secondary contacts'.

HOW OFTEN DO YOU NEED TO ENTERTAIN?

Once again, entertaining your target groups in a number of different ways, over the course of a year, may be more effective than simply holding one annual party. Your most important contacts may need to be entertained frequently – especially if you work in an industry which depends upon a few key contacts, and which exploits personal chemistry to help generate repeat business. For example, you probably take your clients out to lunch, but now is the time to make sure it's timetabled regularly. It starts to sound rather forced, but your clients need never know that you've allocated an annual entertainment budget of three trips to the pub and two smart lunches. Formalizing 'informal' contact in this way makes sure that you really do encourage the relationship, and also means that you spend the same amount of time with each contact – not just those that you get on well with!

WHAT TYPE OF ENTERTAINMENT WOULD SUIT THE NEEDS OF YOUR TARGET GROUPS?

Rather than the actual event, consider more the context. Issues such as the scale of the entertainment, the style, the atmosphere and so on. For example, if you need to entertain an important foreign visitor, then a trip to a sporting event could prove interesting, but rather than hire a marquee and invite all and sundry, keep the guest list to a minimum – yourself, your second in command, spouses and of course your guest and family. Such one-on-one attention would be completely inappropriate for staff, however – they will want to let their hair down and get well away from the work environment. Perhaps a day at an activity centre, riding quad bikes and tanks would prove more appealing? You may need to consider the seniority of your targets as well, considering how best to mix individual groups – an exclusive dinner will suit CEOs, for example, open house at a local pub would be ideal for new trainees.

WHAT'S YOUR BUDGET?

Now you know who you want to entertain, how often, and roughly in what way, you can start to sketch out exactly how much money could be involved – and you'll probably want to reduce it! Of course, this exercise depends greatly upon the size of your marketing budget, and just how beneficial you feel entertaining could be to your business. Make sure you timetable a budget review at the same time as you evaluate the success of the events you've been hosting, so that you can trim or expand the amount of money you allocate.

Insight

Entertaining can take many different forms, with associated budgetary implications, and determining value for money can be difficult. Start with target audience expectations and plan accordingly – you may find that several more modest activities per year could reap just as many rewards as an impressive annual party or day out.

Choosing the right option

Money, as you'll now realize, can prove crucial to the success or otherwise of an event, especially a high-profile occasion. Cost can also raise other, more subtle issues. The last thing you want is for guests to go hungry or thirsty, but if the entertainment is lavish, will it appear too generous? If you are running a service company, will your clients think that you must be charging too much if you can afford to entertain on such a grand scale? Every scenario will be different, so you must use your skill and judgement to assess the impact of what you have in mind – if you are at least aware of these issues then you are more likely to avoid any unpleasant fall-out.

Despite the fear that you have to pull out all the stops, you can achieve good results without necessarily breaking the bank, so let's divide the options by cost to give you some ideas:

LOW-COST

A trip to the pub is probably the cheapest way to entertain a client – and, ironically, can often be the most successful. If this becomes a regular activity, then start to build up a database of places that you know and trust, that can be relied upon to deliver efficient service in a pleasant atmosphere – and make sure you blacklist any that fail. There is nothing more embarrassing than having to wait ages for food that turns out to be indifferent. Pubs which offer both restaurant and bar meal options are good bets, especially those which will allow you to book in advance. A more formal meal can also be a relatively low-cost, but impressive, option especially if you suggest a restaurant with a very good reputation. Once again, at the risk of sounding mechanical, make a note of where you went, and make sure you don't return there every time – unless you are allowing your guest to choose.

Co-hosting an event can also help keep budgets low. If you want to have a drinks party, for example, you could find a complementary organization which may be happy to share the costs of a venue with you, although as most catering companies charge per head for food and wine your final budget will still relate directly to the numbers invited. Obviously, a shared event results in a less exclusive atmosphere, but the opportunity to mingle with groups of new contacts can have its advantages.

Add-on entertaining – associated with a seminar or exhibition for example – is a good way of maximizing both your promotional and entertainment budget. Your venue and invitation costs will already be accounted for within your presentation expenses, so the post-event finger buffet or drinks reception will be cost-effective in terms of both budget and effort. Such entertaining positively attracts delegates to seminars and the like, as they want to take advantage of the networking opportunities on offer, but guests will expect to talk more about business than to generally socialize, so the atmosphere may be less relaxed.

MEDIUM-COST

Medium-cost options include events such as exclusive lunch or drinks parties. As we've already noted, the final cost will depend upon the number of people you want to invite. The venue you choose will be important and can help attract people especially if it's a particularly pleasant or unusual place. Such events may work better if they are linked to a theme or an event, in order to give a *raison d'être* and context. The most obvious, of course, are those linked to seasonal celebrations: Christmas (but diary clashes will be inevitable), Pancake Day, a summer garden party, bonfire night – you'll always be able to find some excuse. Alternatively, is there anything that your organization wishes to celebrate, such as a corporate birthday (ideally a landmark such as ten or 25 years), or the opening of a new facility or building? As with any party, atmosphere is everything, and so you must try and ensure that the setting, the food and guests all combine to create a memorable event. As for all activities, party organizers can be called in if you think you need professional help. They are very useful when it comes to handling all the administrative details, which can be extremely time-consuming, and they have access to a wealth of

contacts – they'll also be able to put forward a host of ideas to
make your party go with a swing.

HIGH-COST

If you are prepared to spend serious money, then you can organize
a truly memorable occasion, and there are endless possibilities from
which to choose – front row seats at a major sporting event, trips
abroad, hot air balloon rides, your own sponsored horse-race,
a truly lavish party. And there are a host of companies ready and
willing to spend your money for you and organize the whole thing
from start to finish.

If you really do want to impress your key contacts, or perhaps
reward your best distributors or employees, then an invitation to
an exclusive or popular event can prove undeniably attractive.
Tickets for the final at Wimbledon, a night at the opera – we can
all think of examples. They will be expensive, but certainly will
be a day to remember. If the occasion becomes a regular annual
event, then it may even become an indirect means of encouraging
loyalty and individuals will actively look forward to their annual
invitation.

However, the 'PR jolly' – where the best seats are snapped up on
behalf of people who don't really have an interest in what they are
about to see – has earned the PR industry, and some of its clients,
a rather unsavoury reputation. But as the reciprocal relationship
between corporate entertainment and event management becomes
ever more closely entwined, then the results are becoming accepted
as a fact of life.

A few basic guidelines

As an event can be an expensive activity it's important to make the
most of the opportunities you are creating. Although everyone will
be having, hopefully, a good time, you will still have to work hard

to make sure your basic aims are fulfilled. The following advice should help:

PLAN METICULOUSLY

As with every other marketing and PR activity, planning is essential to ensure that everything goes smoothly, especially when the occasion is supposed to be relaxed and enjoyable. There are many companies which will handle the planning of such events for you, either independents or associated with a specific venue. Others offer self-contained packages based on tickets to a sporting or other event, and which include refreshments and other diversions. Although expensive, such companies will take away the burden of detailed planning, which would otherwise have to be delegated to a member of your administrative team. They will also provide all the staff needed to run the event on the day, leaving you free to concentrate on your guests.

MAKE SURE YOUR EVENT REFLECTS YOUR CORPORATE ETHOS

This point echoes those made in the chapter on Sponsorship and it's worth saying again. You can use corporate entertaining to underline and strengthen your corporate image. For example, if you are operating in a 'traditional' and perhaps conservative market sector – business advice for example – then a fancy dress party will suit neither your image nor your target audience, which will be expecting an invitation to a cricket match, or a concert. If it's important to stress your imaginative and creative abilities, then apply these to your choice of venue or type of event. Once again, events are supposed to be relaxed, informal and enjoyable so it's important that your audience does not feel uncomfortable by being placed in surroundings in which they feel unsure. Such events may also tie in nicely with any sponsorships you have embarked upon, to reinforce the point that you are supporting local sport or music for example.

PREPARE TO BE ENTERTAINING!

Your guests will expect you to be a charming, courteous host throughout the event you've planned, so mentally prepare for a long stretch of smiling attentiveness! If you know that some of your clients can be hard-going socially, then make sure you have colleagues on hand to take over the reins at certain points. Broadening the invitation to include spouses and partners can help greatly in such circumstances, also increasing the informality and conviviality of the occasion. If you are planning a party, then make sure you invite an interesting mix of people, including some you know are always 'good value' – likewise, make sure that any employees attending can circulate with confidence and are not put off by a room full of people they don't really know. You must also manage a balancing act of talking to the people you really need to impress, whilst making sure that everyone is being attended to – once again, brief colleagues to make sure no guest is left alone.

TEST YOURSELF

The Klipp'ems company is now growing fast – it has a team of reps out on the road, a growing employee base and is hunting for more investment in order to grow into the next stage. Should it be thinking about using entertainment as one of its strategic activities? Devise a plan of action, identifying the different events the MD could consider, the target groups which could be invited, and the benefits it would gain the company.

PR Matrix
Review your Activity column once again – do you need to entertain any of your target groups? Add an appropriate activity to your list.

7

Internal public relations

In this chapter you will learn:
- *why an internal communications strategy is so important*
- *about different strategic activities*

When it comes to listing target audiences, staff are often somewhere near the bottom of the list – if they've been remembered at all. Yet your staff are one of the most important factors in the success of your organization especially if you are a service company, and stand or fall on the enthusiasm and loyalty of your employees. When all your other PR activities start falling into place you'll start to raise expectations, but no matter how good your PR campaign may be, an organization ultimately depends on the actions of its staff. Unless they are as enthused as your customers or clients then the whole business structure can come crashing down. Internal PR can provide some of the glue which can bond an organization together and help sustain this enthusiasm.

An internal PR strategy can be invaluable within your overall PR programme. No matter how few people you actually employ, it's surprising how quickly an individual can start to feel 'left out' of the general news round, even in an office of only three or four, simply because there is no formalized mechanism for internal communications. This problem can become worse if some of your staff (and many do) work from home, are part-time, work away from a desk, phone, or computer, or are simply often 'out and about'. Implemented as part of your overall PR strategy, an internal PR campaign will help give structure to the process of communicating messages within your organization. But it shouldn't simply be regarded as a better way of sending memos – internal PR can also achieve some serious goals:

▶ *Spreading the concept of 'ownership' among staff at all levels, making them feel more involved. The feeling that management is operating an open policy towards information gives out a positive message to all employees.*

▶ *Encouraging staff involvement by creating mechanisms which enable staff to make suggestions and comments both informally and formally.*

▶ *Creating feedback mechanisms which are regular, sustained and accountable, and which show that staff are listened to – rather than simply encouraged to talk.*

▶ *Providing a greater sense of 'unity', especially if you operate from more than one office, have sites overseas, or employ a remote sales force or distributor network.*

▶ *Counteracting the spread of rumour, gossip and – by default – misunderstanding, by providing more information up front, and by disseminating it faster.*

Insight

Management-driven internal PR aims to improve communication between all members of an organization in order to encourage greater 'ownership', thereby improving loyalty and performance. Interaction plays a key role, enabling staff to feel more involved in the strategic decision-making process.

By definition, an internal PR plan needs to be management driven, led (and to a greater extent administered) from the top. So why commit valuable time to such a programme when it could be spent actively marketing your organization? Here are some of the benefits:

▶ *Staff will become committed, active partners in the growth of the organization, feeling that their contribution has made a difference on more than one level.*

- ▶ Clients will receive better service from all employees, if those employees feel more involved in their organization.
- ▶ Mechanisms are put in place for the efficient transmission of information of all types, both positive and negative – staff know where to go to find out information, and in the case of a crisis, such information can be disseminated quickly and efficiently. Rumour – and by default misinformation – will be kept to a minimum.
- ▶ Insecurities and bad feeling resulting from poor or no communication will be kept under control.
- ▶ Good suggestions made by any individual within your organization can be used for the benefit of the whole workforce.

For an internal communications campaign to be successful, however, it demands more than just the will of the PR team – you'll also need to ensure:

- ▶ Commitment from all levels of management – you can't afford to let one of your team leaders or directors opt out from the stated policy once it's put in place. If different staff receive different information, or information of different quality, then the outcome may be divisive and potentially damaging.
- ▶ Individuals at all levels of seniority must be actively encouraged to listen as well as contribute. Internal PR is not just a means of allowing staff to heckle management, but to establish a systematic, two-way flow of information, comment and opinion, for the benefit of everyone, and this flow must be managed effectively in order to avoid accusations of tokenism or box ticking. If you really do want to encourage staff feedback, then your response is a vital part of the loop, if your staff are to feel that the time and effort they spent thinking on your behalf was not wasted. Responding can take time, and so needs forward planning – and this forward planning may prompt you to plan for fewer interactive mechanisms, which will probably be a good strategy if a higher quality of response is therefore easier to maintain.

▶ *Honesty – this really is the best policy when it comes to dealing with staff, as one fabrication or falsification will be remembered forever, and nothing you say afterwards will be regarded without some degree of suspicion. Honesty is your prime consideration when trying to decide what to say and how to say it.*

▶ *A match between external and internal messages. It can prove disheartening and certainly annoying if the public image your employer creates is one which isn't replicated within the actual workplace – or that you cannot deliver promises that external campaigns are making on your behalf. Right from the start, ensure that internal and external messages are consistent, helping to improve the effectiveness of both internal and external strategies.*

▶ *Integration of the programme into the management process. Internal PR should not be an afterthought and a 'bonus' for staff, it should be integral to other management plans and programmes.*

Insight

Assess staff needs, and mechanisms already in place, before identifying key internal PR activities. Many current tools may simply need a review to make sure they meet evolving staff expectations. If interaction is encouraged, plan ahead to ensure resources are in place to manage staff responses effectively.

Planning an internal PR campaign

ASSESS YOUR AUDIENCE

If you want to plan an internal PR campaign, then as with any other activity, it's essential to fully understand your target audience before you begin.

Why not implement a staff communication audit – just as we considered when planning our media campaign? (In fact, the two could be done at the same time.) Such an exercise also makes a good start to the whole programme, demonstrating – by its very existence – the active intention of senior management to search for views and opinions. Of course, its ultimate success does then depend upon action being taken as a result!

A staff communications audit aims to understand and identify the differing needs and attitudes of various staff groups, looking at issues such as their perceived relationship with their employer or with management, and in particular looking at communications issues and the ways in which information is obtained and exchanged both with peers and those elsewhere up and down the management hierarchy. Obviously, the larger your staff base, the more relevant the exercise, as an interesting range of key concerns and issues will emerge from such an analysis, often challenging the set assumptions of your management team. Even though this seems to be an activity more appropriate for a large employee group, even the smallest number of staff – even a single employee – should respond positively to the task of identifying how internal communications could be improved.

When drafting the basic questionnaire, make sure you tailor the questions to meet the more specific needs of different staff groups. Sales reps, for example, will work in a very different manner from the general admin team and so questions have to reflect the ways in which people actually work. It may also be interesting to ask different staff groups how they assume other sections receive information – and check these perceptions against reality.

Depending on the size and nature of your organization, this exercise can be done online, by email, even pen and paper if staff prefer and find that easier. You probably also want to guarantee anonymity if you want an honest response.

IDENTIFY APPROPRIATE ACTIVITIES

Your assessment of the communications mechanisms already in place – whether as a result of a full audit, or simply by summarizing the mechanisms you know already exist – will probably demonstrate that your underlying policy, whether overt or subconscious, has been based more on a day-to-day, 'need to know' approach. This is not necessarily due to management secrecy but more to avoid overloading staff with what you consider to be irrelevant information. However, if it's obvious that things could be improved, you need to identify those activities most appropriate to the nature of your employee base and use them more frequently and more effectively. It's also important to note that your staff will be gaining a lot of their information informally – in the canteen, as office gossip, the corridor meeting. Don't try to ignore or squash these activities – in fact, if the quality of information is generally improved, then it could be that some of these informal mechanisms are just as effective as some of the more formal, and you may want to extend these opportunities, perhaps by providing more spaces or opportunities for staff to interact.

Strategic activities

If you decide that you would benefit from a more structured approach to communications, consider the following activities and select those which will best suit the nature and size of your organization:

MAKE BETTER USE OF YOUR INTRANET

For many organizations, an intranet is the main vehicle for internal communications. Although often used primarily as a repository for essential documentation, increasingly the intranet has become an important internal PR tool at all levels, encouraging communication both from and between management and staff, and between staff members as well. If you already have an intranet, review its use from an internal PR angle. For example, how much internal communication is functional, or repeats what is happening elsewhere? What is the balance between proactive and reactive communications? How much is specifically designed for, and driven by, the functionality of an intranet and the possibilities it offers for interaction – a two-way flow of ideas can be very beneficial for both staff morale and organizational development. An intranet requires ongoing investment and maintenance, so is probably only be feasible if you can justify the spend in more than just PR terms, and it will improve internal communications in ways cannot be achieved using other mechanisms.

INTERNAL PUBLICATIONS AND EZINES

If you feel your organization is of a large enough size to merit the work involved, then a staff newsletter is another good vehicle for circulating general information, and it can even be mailed to wider audiences such as suppliers and distributors. In the past, the cost of printing and distribution has made the staff newsletter an activity only relevant to the larger organization, but the staff ezine is a different matter – quick to set up, fast to disseminate (especially through an intranet) and which can almost be produced on a rolling basis if there is enough content. If you are already publishing an external newsletter, then the editor could also handle the internal version as much of the content may well be similar, especially corporate or staff related news.

However, it's easy for such a newsletter to be seen as a management mouthpiece so staff must be actively encouraged to contribute – this is often easier said than done. One solution is to physically appoint a newsletter representative from each department or team within your organization, making them responsible for a round-up of team news, and for the identification of those individuals who may be able to contribute something more interesting. Staff representatives could even become part of any editorial meetings.

Many of the guidelines for the production of 'market-facing' newsletters (see Chapter 4) also apply to internal publications. In terms of content, however, consider the following:

▶ *Allocate a regular slot to each area of your organization which should be covered to counter any criticism of bias or neglect.*

- Make sure you also have a good balance between business and people news, and that the spread of people featured come from all parts of the organization, and from all levels.
- Try to avoid any editorial bias towards the more extrovert or able members of your organization – you'll probably find that they are the most willing to contribute, but the end result could appear unbalanced.
- Vary the tone of the pieces you include; for example, make sure 'light' pieces are featured as well as more thoughtful articles. Regular columns such as 'Day in the life' or 'My top ten', can focus upon anyone within your organization, from management to shop floor, adding interest for everyone.
- Provide opportunities for feedback in various ways – competitions, quizzes, even a letters page if you think that anyone will contribute!
- Also use the newsletter as a vehicle for any positive feedback received from clients or customers – it's often hard to find suitable methods of circulating this type of good news.
- It's important to remember that staff newsletters or ezines, no matter how limited the circulation, will be in the public domain once published. They will be left around, passed on, taken home, so make sure that the content does not include anything unsuitable for external consumption – and this includes in-jokes and humorous articles, if they may cause offence when taken out of context.

Insight

Remember that not all staff have regular access to a computer, phone or even desk, so make sure your strategy embraces a range of activities. Sometimes the simplest of mechanisms, such as staff noticeboard or space to talk, can be an effective vehicle for disseminating certain information.

PROMOTE EXTERNAL PR ACHIEVEMENTS INTERNALLY

You may have issued a successful press release, been interviewed on TV, or produced a brand new brochure – but have you told all your staff about these and other ongoing PR activities? Keeping staff informed about external communications activities is important. Not only do they then feel valued rather than ignored, but they are also more aware of what the organization is up to within the marketplace, and can therefore speak with some knowledge if ever asked a question by a customer or client about any external activity that might be taking place. Awareness of what is being done may also prompt some additional ideas which could contribute towards the wider PR campaign.

STAFF BRIEFINGS

Most teams will have regular meetings which focus on work – but how often are meetings held which focus on news and information? It's probably not necessary to arrange a special meeting, but instead add a session to the agenda which gives you the opportunity to talk about more general issues, to find out what other members of the organization are up to and for your staff to raise queries or to ask about rumours currently circulating. Alternatively, set it up as a webinar on your intranet, so that all staff can view it at a time convenient to them, and can post questions in advance, with Q&A part of the proposed format. Ongoing online forums can also be used, if you want to encourage longer term, possibly more wide-ranging staff discussion, but again, as well as setting up a mechanism for such activities, make sure you can manage any outcome, whether positive or negative.

NOTICEBOARDS

This may be the most prosaic vehicle but it can be very effective, allowing fast, democratic dissemination of information, especially staff announcements. Depending on the nature of your organization, not every team member may be at a desk or near a computer during their working day, so this additional vehicle may still be one of the most relevant for some. It may seem obvious, but physical noticeboards should be in a venue where all staff will have a chance to see them regularly, and out of date material must be removed promptly otherwise other information is instantly devalued.

SOCIAL NETWORKING TOOLS

As discussed in Chapter 3, social media is becoming (at the time of writing) the next big thing in external marketing and PR, but social networking in particular can also become part of internal PR as well. Some of the biggest organizations are starting to adopt social networking tools for internal communications in order, for example, to help individuals find colleagues with certain skill sets in order to answer specific client needs. Once again, only you can evaluate whether the nature of your organization would benefit from the use of social networking. It can certainly be fast, responsive and (to some) very appealing, but also requires ongoing (perhaps hourly) effort, can be harder to control, and (to others) can be irritating rather than engaging, especially to those without regular online access.

ENTERTAINING

The value of entertaining staff – and the ways in which it can be done – has already been covered in Chapter 6 and it is an important element in an internal communications programme. Remember, however, that if you plan to use entertainment as an activity within your internal PR strategy then the aim is not necessarily to reward individuals for achieving specific targets but to thank them for their hard work, and demonstrate your commitment to their well-being, at whatever level and in whatever job. Try not to restrict yourself just to a Christmas 'do' – there are other times of the year when a social event could lift spirits, and there are also those corporate landmarks which could become a good excuse for a party!

Be sensitive when planning in-house entertaining, however, and make sure it doesn't inadvertently generate negative PR. A high-profile spending spree may not go down well if an office has recently been closed, or a team recently suffered redundancies. It's hard to get the balance right, especially if doing nothing could be perceived as being mean (particularly if profits remain healthy), so take soundings from key staff to determine what would go down well. It may be that smaller team parties – or budgets – work better than a big, corporate bash, for example.

TEST YOURSELF

The Clean Sweeps are doing well – they've expanded rapidly, now
have three separate offices operating in different local towns, and
employ over 100 full- and part-time cleaning ladies, most of whom
work full day shifts out and about in clients' homes and offices.
The management team knows that staff loyalty is vital and wants
to use an internal PR campaign as one of the ways of encouraging
this. What should they do?

PR Matrix
Unless you are a 'one-man band', your staff will certainly be one of
your target audiences. How do you plan to translate the messages
aimed at this target audience into activities? Add these activities to
your matrix.

8

....

Crisis management

In this chapter you will learn:
- *how to develop a crisis management strategy*
- *key preparation activities*
- *what to do when a crisis occurs*
- *about the role of PR in crisis recovery*

Almost daily it seems, one reads about one sort of disaster or another befalling an organization, perhaps not too dissimilar to your own. Product recalls, redundancies, accidents, acrimonious industrial disputes, effects of climate change, damage to reputation by association – there are a host of crises which, if they happened to you, could badly affect your organization, and if you are subsequently perceived as responding badly to the crisis, then the repercussions could be even worse. From the PR viewpoint, 'crisis management' is a structured approach to handling the communications issues that accompany such events, aiming to put in place a strategy designed to direct the right information to the right people with maximum speed, minimizing the risk of misinformation and helping overall damage limitation. The overriding aim is not to hide the truth or dissemble, but to stay in control of communications at a very challenging time, ensuring the correct messages get out.

Effective crisis management is based on advance planning. Of course you can never be sure what type of crisis may occur, or when it's going to happen, but there will certainly be a range of clearly identifiable scenarios (depending upon the nature of your organization and the way in which it operates) which could prompt a crisis. A crisis management plan starts with the active identification of such scenarios enabling you to then establish a range of communications mechanisms designed to manage immediate fallout, helping your staff concentrate on sorting out the core of the problem – the crisis itself. It's important to remember, right from the start, that crisis management is a management-driven communications strategy – although your PRO will advise and implement a lot of the required actions, management must be in control at all times.

Even if you cannot imagine your organization ever needing to plan in such a way, it may still be useful to read through the rest of this chapter. You may start to realize that you are not as invulnerable as you think, and that circumstances may change as your organization grows or develops, making a crisis seem less unlikely.

Developing a crisis management strategy

The following steps provide a basic action plan. This will result in a file of plans, papers and protocols which can be safely locked away, hopefully never to be used. Even so, they should be revisited regularly to make sure details are up to date. Once the plan is complete, you may want to consult your legal advisers, to double-check that anything you plan to do and say at a time of crisis won't get you into even more trouble!

IDENTIFY POTENTIAL CRISES, AND WHO WOULD BE AFFECTED BY THEM

You will already be aware of the type of crises which could affect your organization, and probably have plans in place to deal with the practicalities of, say, a fire, or shopfloor or production problems. Now we need to re-evaluate these crises from a communications point of view, and so planning should start with a structured analysis of all the possible problems that may face you at one time or another – without making yourself either too depressed or paranoid!

Here are a few of the more typical examples. As you'll see, some crises could be entirely your fault, but some will be out of your control, some will be easy to predict, others may hit you out of the blue, and it's also important to remember how the internet, and social media, can rapidly accelerate a crisis, and possibly exaggerate audience perceptions of what's really happening. Horizon watching – the proactive monitoring of developing issues – plays an important role within this preliminary exercise, as it will help identify possible future threats, the speed with which they could have an effect, and review what's happening to other organizations similar to your own.

Insight
Crises can take many forms, and can be triggered by internal events, or by events completely out of your control. Don't get paranoid, but don't think your organization is immune – crisis planning will help you identify what could happen, and plan your reaction accordingly.

Consider, for example:

Internal crises
▶ *Are you a major local employer? Could redundancies have serious local repercussions? Or could possible expansion plans also trigger a major negative reaction?*
▶ *Is it likely that your workforce would ever come out on strike?*
▶ *What would happen if one of your products or services suddenly gave serious cause for concern? Might you ever have to instigate a major product recall?*
▶ *Do you handle or store products or materials that could be dangerous if stolen or misplaced?*
▶ *Do you issue an annual financial statement – what would be the impact if your results were worse than predicted?*

External crises

▶ *Are you associated with products, manufacturing processes or research techniques that could attract negative publicity, for whatever reason?*

▶ *What would be the effect of fire, flood or other serious damage to your property?*

▶ *Would you suffer if a crisis happened to one of your major customers or suppliers?*

▶ *Are there any issues bubbling under at the moment – results of externally commissioned reports or government committees for example – that could have a damaging effect upon your organization if the resulting conclusions went against you or your line of business?*

▶ *Is there an organization similar to your own which is currently attracting bad publicity? Could you be tarred with the same brush if the climate of opinion rapidly changes?*

Preparation activities

Once you've identified the possible crises, then list the audiences that would be affected – customers, clients, staff, shareholders, suppliers etc. The effect on each needs to be considered, an appropriate response drafted and the most suitable mechanism identified – we'll look at a range of specific crisis-management mechanisms in this chapter. The media could play a crucial role in the management of this response phase – at best helping broadcast the information you want to disseminate, at worst provoking or exacerbating a crisis by spreading information which is either untrue, which was not destined for public consumption in an unedited form, or leaking negative information in advance of a carefully prepared announcement.

It's impossible to be too specific about what to do – every industry is different, and every organization will be faced with a different set of challenges, and if you think that crisis management probably should play a more important part of your communication planning, then it's probably time to get in an expert. However, as a starting point, the following ideas provide a basic approach to the construction of a crisis management plan, and will at least get you thinking along the most appropriate lines. First, let's consider what you can do to prepare your organization for the worst:

A CASCADE COMMUNICATIONS PLAN

In the case of an emergency, or if the media are banging on your door, then your most senior staff must be available to represent the company – they will have both the authority to answer questions effectively, and the confidence to manage what could be a very stressful experience. Fielding an untrained, panicking office manager – and it has happened – will only end up sending a host of negative messages to all your target audiences, further compounding the potentially bad publicity brewing as a result of the developing crisis.

But time is of the essence – if a crisis breaks in the middle of the night, when the office is empty, or during a quiet time of year, senior staff may not always be immediately available or on site, when a situation develops. In order to prepare for such an eventuality, create a list of all those who are authorized to speak on behalf of the company in the event of a crisis: the MD or CEO; directors; senior managers; and any other senior staff who are on site most of the time – this may include finance directors for example, or HR managers. Don't forget to include your PRO in the list, as well as any senior consultants you may have working for you – you may even want to include other trusted advisers, such as lawyers or accountants, if you can be confident in their response. Remember that most of the contacts will simply be required to field immediate questions in an intelligent, calm manner, whilst waiting for senior management to become available.

Then create a cascade communications plan, which will enable – if necessary – any individual within your organization to alert the most senior member of staff available. Indicate who should be called first – a line manager or the PRO for example – enabling them to make the decision as to who to contact next, but allow anyone within the organization to initiate the chain. This will make sure you are not left 'speechless' if a crisis starts to unfold.

CRISIS BRIEFING

Obviously, everyone on your cascade list needs to understand what would be expected of them if they were contacted as a crisis was unfolding. Hold a briefing session, to inform everyone of their roles and responsibilities and put systems in place to ensure that everyone is rebriefed (by email or other appropriate means) of any changes that subsequently take place. New recruits must also be included in the loop at whatever level is appropriate, and so your personnel team needs to be involved to ensure that the right amount of information is given to each new appointee.

PREPARE 'HOLDING STATEMENTS'

Once you've identified and documented those who can talk on your behalf, then decide what they can say while you prepare a more detailed response. Unless they are already fully apprised of the crisis, you run the risk of leaving them flapping in ignorance, able only to say 'no comment' – the worst response of all!

This is particularly important if an unexpected crisis hits your organization, as it's often the case that no one knows what is going on – or what will be done – for a significant time, but during this time you may well start to receive urgent calls from a variety of sources, not least the media, all wanting to know what's happening. If you can prepare 'holding statements' in advance – ideally using information drawn from your existing, practical contingency plans – then they can be issued immediately by anyone within your organization authorized to do so. Once again, holding statements will be highly specific to the nature of the crisis you are attempting to contain, but make sure the statement indicates that you are aware of the problem, that you regret any damage or distress that it has caused (if relevant), that you are currently doing something about it and that you will issue a fuller statement at a later time – and if you can indicate an exact time and place then even better. You may have to prepare two or more statements if the crisis will follow a specific event, such as decision by Government or the courts.

Post such statements on your website home page; if you were already well aware that a crisis was about to strike (you have just announced a major round of redundancies, for example) then you will be able to prepare such statements with greater confidence and accuracy, and can already have arrangements in hand for a full briefing session later that same day.

If a crisis does happen, then your most senior staff must be kept free in order to address enquiries from the press or from your most important clients or other contacts (as well as dealing with the crisis itself), but you may also find that your switchboard quickly becomes jammed with calls from a wide range of other individuals, all demanding more information. Therefore, entrust a holding statement to the most senior member of your reception team, who can use it to respond immediately to any customer, client or staff enquiries.

Once drafted, these statements must be kept somewhere secure but easily accessible by the right personnel. Under no circumstances must they be issued accidentally, to the press or to anyone else (thus precipitating a crisis that never would have happened otherwise), or be used by staff members unauthorized to do so.

Q&As

A list of answers to the most likely questions can also prove invaluable (to staff as well to external contacts), and will immediately provide a focused response to immediate queries, and possibly deflect more aggressive questioning at least for a short time. Sketch a draft document for each of your potential crisis scenarios, to provide answers to hypothetical questions – you may also find this exercise useful in making you think more broadly about the possible implications of a crisis situation, and the ways you would deal with it.

Insight

The role of crisis PR is to maintain communications with your audiences, thereby providing clarity, consistency and reassurance. The media can play an important role in crisis development and containment, so building on established media relationships becomes even more important.

PREPARE A CRISIS MEDIA LIAISON STRATEGY

The media will play a vital role in the ongoing development of a crisis, for good or otherwise and whether you want them to or not: the media can even cause a crisis, so it helps if you can encourage them to be your ally right from the start.

Once again, it greatly depends on the exact nature of the crisis as to what you do, but you can certainly start to prepare the ground. For example:

Crisis press contact list

Just as you prepared a cascade contact list for your staff, prepare a list of the most important journalists to contact straight away. Given the fact that most crises are of immediate news interest, your list will probably comprise mainly local or national journalists in print and broadcast media, freelancers, special correspondents and the newsdesks of relevant publications or news services. Your trade press will also want to know more: add weekly publications to the immediate circulation list, and although monthly publications may seem less relevant in the heat of the moment, don't forget to inform them as well. Some leading trade editors are often asked by the daily press to comment on crises, so keeping them informed can be a positive move.

As we have said before, trying to create closer links with local journalists (in particular) can reap benefits during a time of crisis, especially if they have had a chance to get to know your organization and some of the personalities working for it – as a result, they are more likely to be 'on your side' if a serious crisis occurs. If they are also publishing possibly leaked information, a good relationship means that you can call the journalist involved and talk on a more personal level about what has happened, giving your side of the story – if you're lucky, the journalist may even call you in advance, to warn you that the story is about to break. Your aim is to achieve more balanced coverage – if not immediately, at least in the future.

Draft skeleton press releases

Once again, drawing on your list of predicted crises, draft a series of press releases which could be issued as soon as possible after the crisis breaks – as soon as you have something positive or informative to say that is. The press will want to know more, and will need authorized comprehensive information. Once drafted, again, keep these in a secure location, accessible only by your PRO and by senior staff members authorized to approve their issue – it is imperative that such releases should never be issued in error.

Make sure your 'company profile' is kept up to date

General information about your organization can prove invaluable in a host of situations, especially crises. If you are suddenly faced with a barrage of requests for more background details, then having a ready-made, fully approved 'company profile', available online, could be the answer to your prayers. In Chapter 4 we looked in detail at how to prepare such a profile.

MEDIA TRAINING

As a crisis develops, then your senior staff may suddenly find themselves pushed into the media spotlight, and so it's important that they know at least the fundamentals of how to act in such a situation, in order to give them confidence and to ensure their performance is a credit to your organization. We looked at media training briefly in Chapter 3, but if you feel that your organization could be prone to problem situations (if an annual cycle of activity can regularly prompt controversy), then it may be worth investing in training geared specifically to handling crises. During such training sessions, senior staff will experience the type of media attention that a crisis might generate, and will be able to develop the proactive skills required to deal with the media in high pressure situations. Training allows staff to experience the feeling of a telephone or TV interview – invaluable for anyone who has never come face to face with a journalist before. Such training can be expensive, but the knowledge gained by a few key individuals can also be filtered down to other senior team members. Media training companies often employ seasoned journalists used to asking difficult questions, and if you brief them on the type of issue that could affect you, then they can prepare questions which you may not have expected to be faced with, helping your own team enhance its crisis response. It's also worth refreshing media training for senior staff, and if you build up a good relationship with a media training firm, they may be able to step in at short notice and help you prepare for specific interviews, if a crisis is starting to bubble up.

INFORMING STAFF

Staff at every level must be aware of that a crisis management plan exists, in order to make sure that they know what represents a crisis, how to assist your management team, and how to deal with the media on behalf of your organization. Look at your internal PR mechanisms (see Chapter 7), and use those to help inform your staff of the plans you are putting in place, especially those elements which may require their active participation, such as the cascade communications plan. You may feel a more formal approach is necessary in order to underline the importance of abiding by the rules you have established, so it could be part of the induction process, and on your intranet or in your employee handbook.

USING YOUR WEBSITE

In time of crisis your website will become a main point of contact for anyone wanting up-to-date information, and so it's therefore vital that your website is able to respond immediately, in some form or other, to events as they unfold. Depending upon the scale of the crisis, it may be relatively easy to quickly add some new information to your home page (or put up a completely new home page), in order to provide an immediate summary of the situation, an indication of when more information will follow, and any immediate contact details that may be helpful. It may also be wise to suppress certain stories already on your website, especially those which suddenly appear very insensitive, or contradictory. Talk to your IT team or web master as part of your crisis management planning, to establish the best way to manage web content at a time of crisis.

REHEARSE

Once you have your plans in place, then a 'dress rehearsal' may be worth considering, especially if a crisis is not unlikely, and your strategy depends upon a number of staff, possibly in different locations, each with a different role to play. Such an exercise can also show exactly where weak links exist, and which staff still feel under-prepared. If you employ an outside PR agency then use them to help you, as staff often find it easier to 'pretend' or role play with an independent adviser acting as a facilitator, rather than amongst themselves. Once again, specialist agencies exist which can provide specific training in handling crises. Alternatively, you can run through the whole crisis scenario step by step, to identify where the gaps will emerge if the real thing happens.

REVIEWING CRISIS MANAGEMENT PLANS

It's crucial that the plans you have so carefully drawn up remain current and valid. Make sure that whoever is responsible for crisis management planning undertakes a regular review, and that specific triggers are identified which justify an update to plans – staff changes, for example, or changes to product details. Any revisions must be circulated immediately to those who need to know, and the information reiterated within any communication which forms part of the overall strategy.

Implementation

Despite the care you take over your plan, you will, hopefully, never have to use it – although you will find that certain elements (the corporate profile or media training for example) will prove highly useful in other aspects of your work, and it is a lucky organization that continues with no crisis of some sort or another.

If the worst comes to the worst, however, you'll need to put your plan into action. Specific actions will depend entirely on the nature of the crisis facing you, but here's a general summary of what to do:

- *Implement the cascade communications mechanism as quickly as possible – alert all senior staff and make sure they are available in person or on the phone.*
- *If your building has been damaged or destroyed, quickly identify an alternative location as your PR office for the immediate period – this could be the office of your PR consultancy, a sympathetic local business, or even your own home.*
- *Don't panic – whilst assessing the scale of the crisis instruct your PRO to:*
  - *refine and gain approval for the most appropriate holding statements with the most immediate information – issue to all authorized members of staff and release via the website; revise all other documents you have already prepared;*
  - *give a deadline by which more information will be available;*
  - *if necessary make arrangements for the delivery of a press statement – this can be given online, or in person at the front door of your building, within a suitable meeting room or (if your building has been rendered unusable) wherever is most practical;*

> ▷ as soon as you can, revise your press release and email
> it to your press list; include the revised Q&As and
> corporate profile.

As the crisis progresses and hopefully is controlled, issue further
regular statements using all the channels identified in order to
keep your audiences up to date. Monitor ongoing press coverage,
especially if you sense the tide is turning against you – if so, move
quickly to reassure all your target audiences using whatever
evidence you can.

THE ROLE OF PR IN 'CRISIS RECOVERY'

Dealing with a crisis can leave senior management, and the PR
team, exhausted and anxious to get back to the day-to-day routine.
But 'crisis recovery' is a vital phase in the cycle, and PR plays an
important role in restoring your reputation and the profile of your
organization.

Your PR strategy will depend entirely on the nature of the crisis
and resulting impact on your relationship with your target audiences.
If the crisis was outside your control, or even perpetrated against
you (an arson attack for example) then you may find you have a well
of sympathy and support on which you can draw. You need to make
sure this support is not taken for granted, and as soon as the crisis is
under control, you must start to issue positive, reassuring messages
to make sure your target groups need not worry, that jobs or
supplies are not at risk, and that they need not desert you. Making
public your contingency and longer-term plans is an important part
of this, as is a swift return to 'business as usual' PR, with a ready
stream of press releases and other activities taking place.

If the crisis was internal – say a product recall – then the PR
challenge is to rebuild the trust which your target groups may feel
has been abused. You need to acknowledge your problems, and
widely publicize the ways in which the organization has addressed
the causes of the crisis. Your publics need to be reassured that the

same problem can never happen again (to the best of your ability) and that you are willing to admit fault and not hide mistakes.

Crisis recovery PR requires time, energy, optimism and enthusiasm – reserves which you simply may not have. Bringing in an outside specialist at this time may be a good move, although you must be careful not to appear to be wasting resources, especially if the original crisis was fiscal or involved redundancies or strike action. An external viewpoint can deliver illuminating insights into how to go forward, how best to present your organization in the light of what has happened, and how to plan for the longer term.

TEST YOURSELF

You own a firework factory, situated next to a river, employing over 100 local people. The bottom has fallen out of the firework market and the future looks gloomy – in addition, one of your favourite firework ingredients has recently been labelled highly toxic by the European Firework Council and banned from use, even though you still have over 20 barrels of the chemical sitting in a shed in your yard.

What possible crises face you? How should you prepare?

PR Matrix

Crisis management falls outside the remit of ongoing PR as hopefully you will never need to use it. However, if you think that adopting some of the strategies outlined here might be beneficial – or that a full plan may even be necessary – add this to your objectives and set aside a separate strategy development programme for crisis management planning.

9

......

Specialist PR

In this chapter you will learn:
- *about government affairs or lobbying*
- *about financial PR*
- *about PR and price sensitive information*

Most PR programmes operate within fairly modest parameters – target audiences are easy to identify, objectives are clear, and implementation focuses on a range of tried and tested activities. But every now and again you may find yourself needing more specialist advice. This chapter looks at two such PR 'disciplines' – Government affairs, and financial PR – in order to give an overview, and to provide some guidelines on what to do if you need specialist help.

Government affairs or lobbying

If your list of target audiences includes any elected official, at either local or national level, then you could find yourself embarking upon a programme of 'Government affairs' or lobbying. Your main aim is to inform elected representatives of the needs of your organization or your industry, in order to help direct the development of those local or national policies which affect your organization. In business, Government affairs campaigns usually fall under the 'corporate PR' banner, and run in parallel with consumer or trade PR campaigns, taking either a leading or background role as the need arises. For any organization promoting or fighting a particular issue or cause, Government affairs is often the lynchpin of the PR strategy.

Even the smallest organization may find itself launching a Government affairs campaign, albeit a modest one, as a result of one of three main drivers:

To support a trade-driven initiative

All industries have 'issues' – regulatory, legal, legislative – which affect the way an individual business operates. Such issues are discussed and debated at industry-level, but are also raised with Government representatives, mainly through dialogue between the Government and trade bodies, specialist advisers and leading organizations within the industry concerned. If a smaller organization wants to become more actively involved, perhaps for specific business reasons or as a way of raising profile, a Government affairs campaign can provide an effective vehicle, allowing an organization to more effectively join the larger debate whilst lobbying for its own particular cause.

To support or raise awareness of a broader issue

For non-commercial organizations, a Government affairs programme is often essential to the success of an issue-based campaign, and can generate high profile PR opportunities.

Commercial organizations that feel particularly strongly about certain non-business issues sometimes choose to lead the argument from the front and lobby proactively for change. Although the issue chosen will be relevant to their industry, it may also reflect a broader set of values with which an organization wishes to be associated. Championing a 'good cause' may therefore become a PR activity in its own right, and can prove an ideal vehicle for a host of promotional activities, raising profile and enhancing reputation along the way. Supporting a 'non-business' issue does have inherent risks, however – you may find yourself spending more and more money on an activity which is only loosely related to your business goals, and if the issue becomes even slightly controversial you can run the risk of alienating a section of your target audiences, even the Government.

In response to an unforeseen development
The worst-case scenario – to suddenly find that your organization is likely to be at the receiving end of some damaging legislation, or to discover that an issue has suddenly arisen which could prove a serious threat to your livelihood. Under these circumstances, a campaign can be launched with some degree of panic, and lack coherence of both message and effort, vital if it is to achieve both short- and long-term objectives – however, in reality, most campaigns are launched in just these circumstances and still achieve valuable results, so don't be too disheartened if you start your campaign feeling hurried or rushed.

IMPLEMENTING A GOVERNMENT AFFAIRS CAMPAIGN

Government affairs programmes can prove costly, time-consuming and – if the tide of opinion turns against you – potentially damaging, so make sure you use this particular PR tool for good reasons, anchored firmly to your overriding aims and objectives. You may find that you can add little to the work already being done by your trade association, or by a larger, related organization, and so all you need to do is monitor the situation and find opportunities to add support when appropriate.

But if you work within an industry which is continuously beset by issues and debates, a more proactive approach could reap valuable rewards, minimizing potentially damaging developments and raising your profile within target groups as a champion of just causes. Capitalize on any 'horizon watching' activities – proactive monitoring of emerging industry developments – that your PR or sales team undertakes, and identify those issues needing more investigation, so that you are prepared in advance should an issue blow up quickly, or are in a good position to launch a campaign if the climate of opinion is in your favour. At the very least, you can put together a skeleton campaign plan which can be implemented should a serious crisis occur – see Chapter 8 on crisis management for more information.

If you have decided to launch a Government affairs campaign, here are a few golden rules:

▶ *Lobbying is not a restricted practice so if you decide to add lobbying to your list of PR activities, don't assume that you will automatically need the assistance of a specialist consultancy. Generally, politicians and officials want to hear from you and not from a consultant. If you need a Government affairs consultancy it will be for their strategic and technical expertise.*

▶ *If you are responding to an emerging issue, then you must act as quickly as possible, both to try and effect damage limitation and to start what can be a long process as soon as you can. The quicker off the mark the better the results.*

▶ *Always start by going to those who represent you, your Member of Parliament or other elected representative. Not only does this help build bridges with a highly influential member of your local community, but it also serves to hasten the general political process. The best way to begin is by preparing a written outline summarizing the issue or problem as you perceive it, together with your suggested solution. Send this to your MP or elected representative asking them to act upon it and to forward your letter to the appropriate department. Your MP or elected representative should then send on your correspondence with a covering letter – this serves to fast-track your concern, greatly improving the chances of notice being taken. Capitalize upon the contact you have made by keeping them informed of both the progress of your campaign, and of the development of your business in general.*

▶ *In addition, contact your industry trade body or even a local business association such as the Chamber of Commerce, asking them to support you in your fight. Once again, a letter to a Minister will carry more weight if delivered under the banner of a trade organization. Trade bodies are also used to working within the political environment and so will be able to provide good advice on how to achieve your goals.*

▶ Officials must also be approached – many issues revolve around technicalities and detail rather than the broad brush of Government or executive policy, and so a necessary activity is to arrange a meeting between an expert from within your organization and the relevant Government official dealing with the relevant portfolio (the Government department will be able to give you this information). If the issue is current, then civil servants are often very happy to gain a better understanding of the implications of proposed legislation.

▶ As we have already noted, it isn't necessary to use a specialist consultancy, but if a bad decision could prompt a crisis, then hiring such an agency might be worth considering: this is particularly true if the issue facing you has come out of the blue. Professional consultancies should not lobby for you – this role must be left with the senior members of your management team, and to a certain extent to your PRO if he or she is sufficiently experienced. Use your consultant to guide you through all the necessary stages and procedures, to identify the specific levels within Government which you need to influence, and to make you aware of the political nuances which will be in play. This is where they will earn their money, and you must take full advantage of their skills if you choose to use them.

▶ The range of services offered by Government affairs consultants do vary, so before choosing a consultancy, it is important to be clear about your own objectives in order to make the right choice. Most likely you will be looking for strategic advice on who, how and when to lobby, and for technical support in the management of your campaign. This could include, for example, help with research, with the drafting of submissions or amendments to legislation, and advice on the most effective way to make your representations. Whatever the central issues involved in your campaign, you should ensure that the consultancy has experience in handling cases similar to your own and, if it is appropriate, specialist knowledge of your sector. It is equally important to ensure that the consultancy has the necessary staff and resources

to meet your needs. Don't be afraid to ask for references:
a consultancy with a good track record will be more than
willing to provide references from existing clients.

▶ *If, as part of your lobbying activities, you need to gain the*
support of audiences outside the Government circle, then
you need to supplement your Government affairs programme
with a range of associated PR activities. Tailor some of your
ongoing PR to match lobbying objectives – try to place some
discursive or controversial articles within your trade press, for
example, in which you can state your arguments and declare
your support for a particular cause. Host a seminar which
focuses on the issue, or sponsor a relevant event. Websites are
a highly useful vehicle for issue-based PR, as they can be used
to state arguments clearly and concisely, can supply additional
detail at any level required, and can provide up-to-date
progress reports.

However, when integrating your Government affairs campaign
with ongoing PR work, make sure that you continue to work
towards all your stated objectives – you don't want to bore
audiences by always going on about the same issue, or becoming
associated solely with a particular campaign, affecting overall
audience perception.

Insight

If you want to extend your PR campaign to include
Government affairs (or lobbying), or to support an investor
relations strategy (financial PR), then you need specialist
help. Both areas require skill and expertise, and knowledge
of the specific rules (some legally binding) which govern both
areas of activity.

Financial PR

Financial PR specialists talk to two main audiences, the financial
press and city analysts, and focus on two main types of activity,

investor relations and City press relations. Companies can choose to appoint an in-house specialist, or use a consultancy.

As with most forms of PR, the overriding principle of financial communications is that ongoing relationships and a mutual understanding between a business and its key audiences should ensure that its case is both well understood and sympathetically received when it has something important to say.

Companies would certainly be well advised to call upon financial PR specialists if they are considering a listing on a Stock Exchange within the foreseeable future. Although not a mandatory requirement, any company wanting to float will have to issue a variety of press releases and other informative documents and there are strict procedures which govern the way such material is written and distributed, with serious penalties for any transgression. Consultancies, with their extensive experience of the transaction process, can make sure their clients keep on the right side of the law, whilst also honouring obligations and commitments. The vast majority of organizations feel, therefore, that the assistance of a specialist consultancy is invaluable, and is one less thing to worry about at what can be a highly stressful time.

FINDING A CONSULTANT

Finding a suitable consultancy is not difficult; your financial advisers will provide a number of recommendations, selecting agencies with a good track record and with specific experience either in your market sector or of handling companies similar to your own.

As you start your selection process you may find that a recommended consultancy is already working for a direct competitor – but whereas this would be a serious concern if you were planning a consumer or trade PR campaign, within the more rarefied world of financial PR this is less of a worry. Financial consultancies are limited in number, and if a consultancy specializes in a certain industry sector, then it will invariably be working for organizations similar to your own.

Timing will be the issue, rather than a conflict of professional loyalties – if a direct competitor is planning to float at around the same time as your organization, then don't share consultancies.

One of the most important selection criteria is that the client–consultant relationship is a good one – even if you feel that you have no way of judging whether one consultancy is better than another, gut instinct and personal chemistry will help you decide. You are about to embark upon a very intensive period of co-operative endeavour and so it's vital that you get on well with the personalities involved.

FINANCIAL PR CAMPAIGNS

Your financial consultant will help you to brief city analysts on the nature of your organization, using information prepared by them but signed off by you. Such meetings are heavily regulated by the Stock Exchange to ensure that information is released in an orderly way so that no unfair advantage can be gained by any one individual. The consultant will aim to generate an 'exit survey' as a result of these meetings, in order to give you some indication of the feeling within the City about your forthcoming flotation.

Financial PR consultancies are in daily contact with the financial media, who are becoming increasingly important and influential in the City. In terms of media work, the objective is to feed quality stories to key financial journalists, and also to those journalists interested in your particular industry sector. Your consultant will be constantly looking for stories, especially relating to your company accounts, which will be of particular interest to potential investors. As well as financial information, such as business results, stories which can demonstrate industry trends will also be placed, to help give a fuller picture of your organization, its status within your industry, and of the value it represents.

Your relationship with a financial PR consultancy is often short-term and highly intensive, but many consultancies are retained by their clients following a flotation, and are brought in to handle major financial announcements or other relevant issues. They can also play an important role in corporate PR strategies, bringing a City perspective to the development and implementation of any longer-term programmes.

PR AND PRICE SENSITIVE INFORMATION

Although the media has always played a role in the rise and fall of share prices, regulatory authorities are now keeping an even closer eye on the impact news coverage might have on market value. As a result, there is an increased burden of responsibility placed on listed companies to understand the potential effect of anything they say – in press releases, newsletters, websites or 'off the record/off the cuff remarks'. This responsibility may also extend to organizations supplying or dealing with a listed company in any way. So even if you are a small supplier, be very careful if you're handling information from a listed company provided for your own PR purposes – say for a case study or a press release.

Regulatory attention is focused primarily on price sensitive information. This is information which could – if in the 'public domain' – lead to a substantial movement in the value of a share price, with 'substantial' often defined as being 10 per cent or above. Of course price sensitive information is issued all the time: profit warnings, unexpectedly good results, mergers or acquisitions, even appointments to the board can affect share prices for better or worse. But 'official' information of this nature is usually issued under closely controlled circumstances, and in such a way as to meet stock exchange guidelines. Again this is best handled by a specialist financial PR firm.

But what if a journalist gets news of a story that might damage or inflate a company share price? Or what if a member of the management team unwittingly 'lets something slip'? How should a company respond to the press speculation that might result? Once again – get the financial specialist in straight away as the wrong response could be a very serious mistake. Official advice is to say 'no comment' when a journalist presses for 'unannounced' price sensitive information. Although 'no comment' is often anathema to the PR professional (see pages 65–66) it is the safest option in a situation such as this. But a journalist will know that there is rarely smoke without fire and will be loathe to let a potentially good story go so easily. If there really is 'something going on' and it's clear that the media have enough information to put together a broadly accurate story, then it's far better to seize the initiative and, under the guidance of your specialist adviser, issue a formal statement as soon as possible.

TEST YOURSELF

As you'll have gathered, you'll only ever need these types of specialist PR if a very specific set of circumstances arises, or if you are actively involved in the championing of specific causes, so a dedicated exercise is less relevant. However, if either scenario is part of your overall business objectives, then lobbying or financial PR may need to be considered and added to your Matrix.

10

PR professionals: consultancies, in-house, and how to launch a PR career

In this chapter you will learn:
- *when to use a PR professional*
- *how to find the right one*
- *more about PR as a career*

If your PR campaign is proving so successful that your resources are starting to buckle under the strain, or you already know that you'll need specialist advice in order to run your ideal programme, then you have to consider hiring professional help. Your main options are to employ an in-house PR officer, or PR team, pitching the appointment to suit the level of expertise you require, or to hire an external consultant or consultancy. In this chapter we look at each of these options in more detail.

As you learn more about PR, and meet more PR professionals, you might become interested in developing your own career in the PR industry – and at the end of this chapter we'll look at the opportunities available in PR and consider ways in which you can exploit your experience to date.

Insight
If you need professional PR help, you can either employ a PR consultancy, a PR freelance, or hire an in-house PRO or team.

Determine the level of resource and skill required, depending on the ambitions and budget of your PR campaign, before researching the options further.

What type of PR help do you need?

PR help comes in three main forms:

PR CONSULTANCIES

Operating as independent agencies, sometimes as part of a national or international group, consultancies offer dedicated PR expertise, often within a particular industry sector or discipline. Consultancies can bring the advantages of manpower and specialist knowledge available as and when you need it. Using a consultancy can be expensive – their average annual fee may equal the salaries of two in-house professionals – and so this option is probably only worth considering if your campaign requires a significant input of time either for a limited period (a launch phase for example), or you want to invest in PR by implementing a wide ranging PR campaign and sustain this over the longer term. Administration and management of the 'client–consultant relationship' can represent a significant part of consultancy start-up costs, and so the longer you maintain the relationship the more productive the outcome will be.

Consultancies can deliver significant manpower, both in the day-to-day running of your PR programme, and if a major event demands a number of extra, experienced hands. A consultancy will also handle all programme administration which, as we've already seen, can prove very time consuming and laborious. But one of the most important advantages is that a consultancy has the time to think proactively on your behalf, and to apply its creative skills to your PR campaign. It also has access to and knowledge of a wide range of PR resources and media and other contacts, including access to more specialist advisers in other branches of PR.

Every client on a consultancy's books is termed an 'account' and, depending upon the amount of work involved, a team of PR professionals will be assigned to each account, to ensure that there is always someone fully briefed on your PR programme and able to provide answers to immediate queries. Account teams often comprise an Account Director or Manager, who manages the PR programme, and an Account Executive, who handles day-to-day administration, and they in turn will be supported by administrative assistance. Additional levels of seniority also exist, but it depends upon the size and organization of the consultancy as to the nature of the hierarchy in place.

One common criticism of consultancies is that clients often feel that they spend most of their time speaking to the account executive, the most junior member of the team, than working with the senior consultant who persuaded them to hire the consultancy in the first place. There is also the problem of team changes as consultancy staff change jobs or move on, taking their accumulated expertise with them.

The reverse is equally true – consultants find it difficult to run a programme when they only have access to junior management, having worked primarily with senior staff during the programme development phase. If only junior management remains closely involved then important, strategic decisions and top-level approval can be delayed, and if the decision-making skill of a junior manager is doubted by a senior consultant (as can often happen) then the whole relationship can be difficult. The overriding aim of a PR programme is to communicate the essence of your organization, and it's therefore vital that senior staff remain closely involved in the ways in which this communication is managed and implemented.

PR consultancies also come in other forms. For example, a number of consultancies comprise only freelancers who come together for certain projects, but who remain self-employed. This business model can deliver breadth of experience as and when required, and can prove more cost effective than a full scale PR agency, especially if your needs differ from month to month. In addition, such 'associates' tend to be older or more experienced in what they do, and will tend to stay with the client for the long term, as they won't necessarily be looking for another job or for career progression, as junior staff in many traditional PR consultancies tend to do.

'Full service' marketing agencies also often offer PR – depending on the size of the agency, they can provide a fully resourced PR service, equivalent to that on offer from a dedicated PR consultancy, PR skills from a smaller team, or the services of an individual PR practitioner (sometimes a freelance, working for the agency). If you only require limited input, then PR provided in this way can prove more cost-effective than using a PR consultancy, and the resulting campaign should integrate fully with other marketing activities (such as advertising) if the agency is handling these for you as well.

Retainer agreements and project fees
Most consultancies want to establish a 'retainer' agreement, a regular commitment from each client to use the agency for so many hours per month, or for a set fee, based on the scope and nature of the campaign. If you go ahead with such an arrangement, then you are committed to paying this amount every month, plus additional expenses and other costs depending upon the nature of the activities undertaken. This enables you to budget for PR with more accuracy, but also represents a financial commitment, which you must make sure you make the most of.

Many agencies are equally happy to charge by the project, although this is more relevant to discrete activities with a specific end point, such as a product launch.

Managing a consultancy
Don't think that hiring a consultancy will relieve you from all PR responsibilities – the relationship needs to be managed, and depends quite heavily upon the involvement of your senior staff in order to brief the consultancy of new developments, approve actions, take strategic decisions and act as spokespeople for your

organization (we'll look at these responsibilities in more detail later in this chapter). It's not uncommon for consultancies to be under-used, simply because their client can't find time to provide sufficient input to keep the programme running. A good consultancy should flag such problems fairly readily, but it is important to be aware of the commitment you will need to make to the relationship before you embark upon it, and before you become disillusioned with the results of your investment in PR.

Conversely, you may overuse your agency, particularly during the first few months of your campaign activities – most consultancies tend to take the longer view during this period, and assume that the workload will even out, but they will also point out if this overwork is consistent and either suggest a period of 'rest' so that the balance is restored, or that you increase your budget and hire more of their time.

INDEPENDENT CONSULTANTS

Many PR professionals turn freelance and become independent consultants, offering advice or input at a variety of levels. Many specialize in a particular field (often based on their personal career experience), whilst others offer an all-round capability.

An independent consultant can be more cost-effective for a smaller organization, although as they can only offer their time and expertise they will not be able to provide either continuous availability or access to the resources that consultancies offer. Once again, depending upon the nature of the assistance you require, freelances can be hired project by project, or you can decide upon a longer-term relationship, including them within your strategy and relying upon their input over a sustained period of time. Freelance consultants often become regarded as part of a marketing team, and gain a thorough understanding of the dynamics of an organization and the market sector in which it operates. As a result such a relationship can run for many years – and I speak from personal experience!

On the other hand (and loath though I am to say it) a consultant working alone can often find it difficult to generate new ideas year after year, simply because they have worked so closely with their client for a long period of time, and because they can't bounce ideas off other members of a team. For these reasons it might be useful to employ an agency from time to time, simply to breathe new life into an ongoing campaign.

IN-HOUSE PRO

Deciding whether or not you need to employ an in-house PRO depends greatly on the scope of your PR campaign – the level of expertise which you think you require, and the amount of administrative support needed, both to run the programme of activities and manage the feedback it prompts. The cost of hiring an agency compared to a new member of staff can make the employment of a dedicated PRO suddenly seem very attractive, especially if you know that PR will play an integral role in your ongoing marketing.

It's worth remembering that your in-house PRO need not be a senior member of the team. As we've already seen, a lot of PR requires basic administrative and project management skills, and it's often these which are in shortest supply. Appointing the equivalent of an Account Executive, for example, will give you someone with a good combination of basic PR understanding and administrative experience. PROs can also play very senior roles within organizations – even at board level.

Another alternative is to employ your PRO either as a part-timer, or with PR as only a part of their overall responsibility. Although this is often the most common option especially when using PR for the first time, it does have serious drawbacks. PR must be proactive as well as reactive – time needs to be spent identifying possible new PR angles or opportunities, and if your PRO's other responsibilities become too demanding then this valuable thinking and planning time soon drops to the bottom of the agenda, or is forgotten completely.

Of course, you don't have to choose exclusively between the options listed above. A combination may provide a successful and possibly more cost-effective solution, enabling you to avoid committing too many resources in one direction.

For example, employing a junior in-house PRO with a senior level freelance consultant could result in good management of strategic direction with adequate administrative support. The junior could benefit from the consultant's expertise, whilst the company would only hire the senior freelance when needed. The reverse of this arrangement could also prove valuable – senior skills brought in house, with lower level administration bought as needed.

Consultancies can be hired on a project-by-project basis if required, which may prove more cost-effective than embarking on a long-term relationship, although in-house support will be required in order to manage the relationship. Bringing consultancies – or consultants for that matter – in on short-term projects also gives you the chance to assess how good they really are before considering offering them a longer-term contract.

Insight

As with any other professional service, reputation, knowledge and experience are important criteria when determining who to supply PR expertise, whether you are hiring an external or internal PR resource. Exploit personal recommendation, as well as unbiased research, to help make your choice.

Finding help

It's all very well deciding that you need PR help, but trying to find the ideal PR partner can be a rather laborious business. Let's look again at the three main categories and see how the process works.

FINDING A CONSULTANCY

PR consultancies can be found all over the country – a quick look online will soon show just how many there are in your local area, never mind the more specialist agencies which may be further afield. It certainly isn't the case that you have to go to a major city to find the best consultancies (unless you require more specialist advice, of the kind we covered in Chapter 9), but even local options may prove confusingly broad. Here are some useful starting points to help you in your search:

Professional bodies and advisers
The UK PR industry boasts two main professional associations, the CIPR (the Chartered Institute of Public Relations) and the PRCA (the Public Relations Consultancy Association). Both run 'matchmaking' services, providing lists of member agencies which meet basic selection criteria, but it must be remembered that the results will necessarily be selective as not all consultancies are members of either organization.

If you are hunting for a more specialist agency, then your own industry trade body may be able to advise on the best-known consultancies in the field. For local advice, ask business advisers – accountants, bank managers, management consultants etc. – they often know the best local service companies around. If you are already using another marketing service such as a designer, copywriter or marketing agency, then they will also be able to help you. PR is often part of a 'marcomms' remit, and such agencies often recommend their clients to buy in this more specialized service as and when it's required, unless, of course, they supply it themselves.

Word of mouth
Most service companies know that recommendation is one of the best ways of generating new business, and PR consultancies are no exception. Ask around in your own local business community and find out who is using whom. Those local marketing seminars, business events (such as those run by the Chamber of Commerce)

or other gatherings and networking opportunities (so highly recommended by PR professionals!) are also another good opportunity to gather opinion and advice. And of course, if your local PR consultancies are worth their salt, you should already know about them through their own PR campaigns!

HIRING A CONSULTANCY

As your list of likely consultancies starts to grow, you need to start applying a few selection criteria in order to help filter the options. Consider:

Location
Would a local agency be more suitable, perhaps because your target audiences are primarily local, and knowledge of the local business community would be an advantage? There is also the added benefit of proximity – you can visit your advisers easily, and they are on the spot should an urgent issue arise.

Speciality
Would you prefer a consultancy that already works for related companies within your particular industry? Using such an agency can reap valuable benefits: they'll already be very familiar with your target media, and have a thorough understanding of the drivers affecting your industry. You may even find that you can take advantage of economies of scale, if your PRO can attend a trade fair on behalf of a number of related clients, then your particular share of the cost can be reduced. However, you do need to be careful about conflicts of interest – make sure that the consultancy isn't already working for a competitor organization, although it should advise you of any problems it can foresee. You'll be lucky to find a specialist agency on your doorstep (although many consultancies offer a skill set which reflects the needs of the local economy – technical agencies often flourish near hi-tech clusters, for example). If specialist help is what you need, you may have to balance the (hopefully) improved results such a consultancy can deliver against possibly higher cost, and reduced personal access requiring more forward planning when meeting.

Size and resources

As soon as you start to research PR agencies, you'll soon find that some are very small and some employ hundreds of staff in locations around the world. For some clients, size and resource is important, and the knowledge that they can take advantage of an international presence is invaluable especially if they are launching an international campaign. If you are planning only a modest campaign – and only a modest spend – then you may feel that your small account would be lost in the corridors of such an agency, and perhaps feel that a smaller consultancy would suit both you and your organization better.

Experience

Perhaps one of the most reassuring criteria is the knowledge that a consultancy has worked on similar accounts in the past, even if it brands itself as a general consultancy. Experience of working with organizations similar to your own brings an immediate appreciation of the internal and external dynamics at play. The agency may even be working with complementary organizations, which will ensure current knowledge of the relevant media, therefore increasing the effectiveness of your PR campaign.

HOW TO SELECT A CONSULTANCY – THE COMPETITIVE PITCH

You may find the selection process relatively easy, and find that you can make your decision simply by visiting a few local consultancies. However, if the decision is not that easy, if your PR budget is considerable, or the outcome crucial to your short- and long-term goals, then it may be worth inviting two or three consultancies (or possibly more) to a competitive pitch. In practice, many organizations invite both specialist and general agencies to pitch against each other, in order to weigh up whether a local agency could deliver as good a service as a remotely located specialist consultancy. From the consultancy's point of view, the competitive pitch, though an essential part of the PR business, is time-consuming, expensive and uncertain, and will only be considered if worth the possible outcome. You don't want to earn a reputation for wasting time.

If you have decided that a pitch is the best way to go forward then the following guidelines may prove helpful:

Initial assessment

Once you have drawn up a shortlist of suitable consultancies, visit their offices to gain some initial impressions. Find out more about the consultancy, and confirm in your own mind that they could work effectively for you. Of course you need to provide a very basic summary of your needs – if nothing else, you need to eliminate the risk of a conflict of interest – but save a fuller brief for later: the desired outcome at this point is a mutual interest in going further.

Briefing

The consultancies will ask for a formal briefing ahead of any pitch, either in writing, at a meeting, or both. Try to make sure that the briefing you give each consultancy is essentially the same – although the way the briefing develops once an agency starts to ask questions is, however, another matter, and will inform your final opinion of the consultancy, the skills of its individuals, and the way it operates.

Make your brief as comprehensive as possible. It should cover company background, current marketing context, and the fundamental reasons why you've decided to use PR, or why you have decided to use a consultancy. You should also discuss your perception (or knowledge) of competitor activities and how successful or otherwise they've been. And last but not least, provide an outline – as you see it – of the aims and objectives of your PR campaign. Most agencies will refine this further to enable them to draw up a full strategy.

Budget

The issue of budget is a tricky one: you may know exactly what you want to achieve, but need to find out how much a consultancy will charge; or, you may have a fixed budget in mind and would rather see what an agency can do within those budgetary constraints. If your budget is relatively fixed, then the latter approach is probably the fairer one, and it often forces a consultancy to be more creative.

The proposal and presentation

A consultancy will expect to respond to a pitch by writing a proposal and then (usually, but not always) presenting this to you and your senior colleagues, and it's up to you how formal you wish the presentation to be. There are no fixed rules, but the more formal the occasion the more serious the atmosphere, and usually the larger the budget.

At the presentation, you want to gain a good idea of the approach the consultancy would take when handling your account: the type of activities it would recommend; the team that would be working with you; and their response to any specific issues raised in the brief. Overall, you want to know that all the points raised at the briefing stage have been addressed, and to be able to judge whether or not the agency has fully understood the nature of your organization and the context in which it operates. You'll also expect to hear reasons why the consultancy thinks it is ideally suited to handling your account, and to gain a fuller picture of the way in which the agency operates – its company history, its current and past client list, its specialties, and the credentials of the proposed account team. This meeting is also a chance for you and your colleagues to ask lots of questions, so make sure you make the most of the opportunity.

Don't expect the presentation, or the accompanying document, to deliver a fully detailed breakdown of the activities your proposed campaign will comprise. These ideas are the consultancy's 'product' and they are understandably reluctant to give them away for free.

Confirming the appointment

After the pitch, try to reach a decision as quickly as possible. Not only will it be easier to make a judgement when impressions are still fresh, but it is also fairer on the consultancies you have asked to pitch. Once you have appointed the consultancy of your choice, let the others know that they were unsuccessful, and provide feedback if asked. It's often very useful for an agency to know the reasons why they didn't get the business, especially if they thought that their presentation went well.

You'll now move into the realms of formal contracts and signed agreements. Make sure a review period is included – if things do not go as well as you hoped, then you may wish to run the whole exercise again, possibly inviting the current incumbent to re-pitch against those less successful last time around.

FINDING AN INDEPENDENT CONSULTANT

Although freelance PR advisers abound, finding a good one can prove remarkably difficult. A single person does not need a lot of business in order to fill up their time completely and, of course, the good ones will always be busy and will not need to advertise, whilst those with plenty of time to spare may either be inexperienced, starting out or simply not very good!

Finding a freelance or one man band is relatively easy – any quick web search will quickly throw up a daunting list of people with apparently very similar skills. However, just as you would when searching for a consultancy, talk to professional bodies, and gain recommendations from advisers or other suppliers, to narrow your search. Many freelances work with designers and marketing agencies, so that is a good place to start, as well as asking other marketing managers you may know. Local business advisers are often aware of local independents, and some business advice services run contact databases which can provide useful leads. Specialist recruitment agencies also exist which can help you find a freelance, or you could even place a recruitment advert, as this would also provide a list of good alternatives, useful if your first choice proves unsuccessful, or if you find the workload is too much for one person to handle.

APPOINTING AN IN-HOUSE PRO

As outlined on page 27, you must decide the level at which you want your PRO to operate, and whether you are happy to appoint someone who will need training or would rather hire proven skills and expertise up front. Whatever the level of appointment you decide to make, ensure that the person you choose for the job already has good writing skills, is a good administrator and is 'media aware' – or at least has the potential to acquire these attributes. Although experience of your industry sector would be an advantage, a general all-round knowledge of PR is more valuable.

Insight

A dedicated PR resource may demand more – not less – of your time, but at a more executive level. Be prepared to support your PR team by sustaining your strategic involvement in campaign activities, as neglect can result in a faltering campaign which makes limited impact.

Managing your professional PR resource

Employing dedicated PR help does not mean that you can forget about PR. In fact, you may find yourself being even more actively involved than before, although hopefully at a more executive level. Your input will still be vital at a number of different levels:

REGULAR STRATEGIC INPUT

You must be prepared to devote regular time to the PR programme at the strategic level. PR administration usually focuses on a regular meeting, usually monthly, with additional meetings as necessary to concentrate on particular issues or activities. At this main meeting, you want to gain an overview of ongoing progress, identify any problem areas and help identify new directions in which activities could move – although you can expect your team to advise you on strategy and tactics, you will still be required to provide the fundamental steer which will ensure that the programme remains on track. You need to let your team know of any new developments – both internal and external – which may affect the way your PR campaign progresses, as only you can judge the potential importance of these developments and advise on the level of response required.

APPROVAL OF PR MATERIAL

Most PR activities result in the production of written material
destined to appear in the public domain – whether in the media,
online, or as a piece of corporate literature. It's very important
therefore, that nothing is issued which does not have the full
approval of a senior manager, as well as the approval of any third
parties that may have been mentioned in the text (see page 86 for
more on this). A fully documented, agreed approval process is
fundamental to the whole PR process but depends entirely upon
your availability to read and approve the material produced. If you
know that you will not always be able to turn material around fast
enough – especially when deadlines are tight – then name other
colleagues who can act on your behalf.

KEEPING LINES OF COMMUNICATION OPEN

Trust is vital. If you want your PR team to operate to the best of
its ability, it needs to be given the full story about any project or
product it is working on – hidden agendas included – and to be
kept up to date with any changes to policy, timing or strategy.
Remember, you've given your PR team the right to speak on your
behalf and if messages change behind its back then the team will
feel exposed, embarrassed and will find it difficult to trust you.

Your PR team needs to feel part of your organization. This is
especially true for external PR consultants, who need access to any
relevant internal circulars or other documents, to your intranet
and other resources as necessary, and who must be allowed regular
communication with any managers or executives designated to
help. Lack of communication can stall a PR campaign in its tracks,
and will prevent a consultancy from doing its job, but not from
charging its fees, as it will have reserved the time needed for your
project in advance.

AS A SPOKESPERSON

Ideally your team does not want to speak for you, although they
often have to in the course of their work. Their aim is to act as an

interface between you and your audiences: when actual comment is required, or expert information sought, then you should be the one to provide the answers. Be prepared, therefore, to speak on behalf of your organization whenever necessary – from providing a journalist with background information for a press release, to introducing or giving a seminar. If you know that your availability may be limited, name colleagues who can also step into this role. If you have put together a 'guide to expertise' (see page 56) then you will already have a list of experts, but you will have to provide additional guidance on who can be trusted to speak on behalf of the organization as a whole. Your crisis management strategy (see Chapter 8) will also have produced a list of approved spokespeople.

AS A JUDGE OF OPPORTUNITIES

Not all PR opportunities can wait until a scheduled meeting in order to be actioned – and an active PR team will constantly be on the lookout for opportunities which could work in your favour, or may be presented with ideas which may need a swift response. Once again, although your PRO can advise on the merits or otherwise of taking advantage of an unexpected opportunity, they will still need access to a senior manager to get the go ahead – especially if the decision has a budgetary implication.

TO EVALUATE ONGOING PERFORMANCE

You are the ultimate manager of the PR strategy and need to be aware of its progress and its success or otherwise. You also need to assess the effectiveness of your team or your consultants. We'll be looking at evaluation in more detail in the next chapter, but it's important to note here that effective evaluation still remains your responsibility.

....
Insight
PR has become a very popular – and competitive – career path, but PR professionals come from all different backgrounds. Core skills are essential, however, and work experience highly valued, so build these up while exploring career opportunities either within a consultancy, or in-house.
....

A career in PR

As more organizations in every sector grow to appreciate the benefits of PR, so the PR industry is growing in response. As a result, there is increasing demand for experienced PR professionals both in-house and in agencies – but there is also fierce and growing competition for every job opportunity that comes along. So how can you launch a PR career?

When giving PR career advice, it's very hard to generalize. Some PROs start their careers straight from college, having gained a PR degree; others gain a diploma or more specialized professional qualification; some work their way up through the marketing department; and others move into PR from completely different sectors of industry, or with completely unrelated experience, having found that they have a talent for communicating the complexities of that industry to the media. There are PR generalists, able to apply themselves to any subject, and PR specialists, working in highly prescribed fields from which they rarely stray. Many PROs are former journalists, sought after for their knowledge of the media and for their ability to write.

It's also interesting to note that PR is a profession in which women are well represented at all levels, and which lends itself to freelance or part-time careers as it is so often project-based, which makes it very attractive for those who plan to work part-time in the future, perhaps to retain their work–life balance. It's also a profession as well represented in the regions as it is in the capital. Given the personal nature of PR, firms usually want to use PR consultancies on their doorstep, rather than have to travel. For the same reason, many of the larger PR consultancies have regional branches.

These days, many PROs are educated to degree level, often in the arts or humanities, or in PR or a related subject, although it's not always essential to have a PR degree or other qualification in order to get your first job. Your degree could even be in the sciences – with the rapid growth in sectors such as biotech or IT, degree-level scientific knowledge is often essential if you want to practise PR in these sectors.

If you want to consider a PR career, most important of all is real – and proven – ability in the core skills essential to PR work at all levels. These include (in no particular order):

An ability to communicate

PR involves talking to and communicating with people all the time – with the media, target audiences, clients, colleagues, employers, suppliers and contributors. It's not a job for anyone who is shy, who finds it hard to explain themselves, or who finds it difficult to be assertive! PR is all about 'getting the message across', so you must be able to work out the best way to do this, and then to do it well.

A talent for writing

You must be able to write effective copy for a variety of media – newspapers, websites, video scripts, brochures, datasheets and so on. As we've already learnt, PR is all about effective communication, and good writing plays an important part in almost all communication activities. 'A way with words' is not something everyone has, and which is the reason why so many people employ others to write for them.

A real interest in the media

Press work is the backbone of PR, and so you must have a keen interest in the way all different types of media work if you are to perform your job well. Being 'media savvy' in general is a great asset, as you need to know how to present information so that the media can make good use of it.

Awareness of current events

A good general knowledge of current affairs is invaluable in most aspects of PR, as you often need to look for the topical 'hook' which will make your story irresistible to the media. It also helps you when proactively planning future opportunities.

An analytical, strategic mind

PR is often about problem solving: you want to achieve a specific objective, so you must identify the best tools to use and the best way to deploy them. As much as anything, you are a professional adviser, providing your client or employer with a plan of action. You must be able to analyse challenges, think strategically, and have a clear idea of what you're doing and why – both when you have time to think and when you're under pressure. This is particularly valuable in agency work, where you will be asked to apply your PR knowledge in a wide range of different contexts, often for more than one client at a time.

Good organization

PR can be very fast-moving and demanding. Deadlines drive everything, and unexpected opportunities can result in lots of work at very short notice, on top of an already heavy schedule. Most PROs thrive on pressure, which gets greater the higher they go. But you need to be super-organized in order to keep on top of every aspect of the PR campaign, good at planning ahead to make sure things are done on time, and also able to follow up activities in order to judge how well they went.

A flexible approach

PR can be very unpredictable, and although you may plan every action down to the last detail, you must also be able to carry on when events take a different turn. Some people can't cope with this level of uncertainty, or lack the ability to think on their feet and change plans in order to get the job done. Depending on the business sector, in-house PR tends to be less volatile than agency work, simply because there's only one client, and a lot more work is proactive rather than reactive. But that's not to say that a sudden press opportunity may need urgent attention, or an issue or other story may suddenly break, demanding an immediate response. If you work in an agency on more than one client account, then this type of situation can easily multiply. In an agency, of course, you can draw on a team of PR professionals who can help out, but nevertheless, it helps if you thrive on unpredictability!

IN-HOUSE OR CONSULTANCY?

If you want to work within PR then the options are in-house or consultancy, with freelance a longer term option, only for the more experienced.

Consultancies (especially the larger firms) tend to offer more entry-level opportunities simply because they employ more dedicated PR staff, but as we've already noted, agencies vary hugely in character, from the huge multinational to the very small, the very regional, or the very specialized.

Larger agencies obviously offer more opportunities (although each vacancy is still highly contested), with some offering graduate training, and also internships (see later in this chapter for more detail). But as a junior you'll be a very small cog in a very large machine – although you'll learn a lot you might feel that your influence and impact is very small, and it might be some time before you feel you can really make your mark.

Smaller agencies demand more versatility from their staff and you may find yourself helping run the business as well as your client accounts. Although a fantastic place to learn, smaller agencies usually want a bit of experience from the people they hire, especially if they want someone who can start earning fees immediately, and because they are simply less able to provide dedicated training.

Larger agencies offer a clear progression route for ambitious PROs, with responsibilities expanding as they rise up the ladder. Senior

PROs in big agencies command quite significant salaries, although these also come with the biggest workload and the greatest level of stress. Career progression in a smaller agency is usually fairly obvious from the day you start – and if you come in at a senior level, there may be no obvious progression at all, although your seniority will increase as the agency grows (if more junior staff come in below you) and your salary is often more closely linked to the success of the agency. The type of work you do will also depend on the type of client accounts the agency wins. There will be no opportunity to move around departments to gain experience in different sectors, and so you may feel your ambitions are restricted. But by the same token, no two days in a smaller agency will be the same, and there is no knowing what the next phone call will bring!

As a rule, there are fewer in-house opportunities for entry-level PROs, as only the largest organizations have dedicated in-house PR teams, but if you live in an area with a lot of small businesses, you may find more opportunities. More often, one individual, usually within the marketing department, is primarily responsible for PR, perhaps with a marketing junior to help with administration. An in-house PRO usually has to have experience in order to do the job, especially if they are the only one in the organization with PR responsibility. However, it's perfectly feasible for a junior marketing assistant to hope to move into PR, especially if they show a talent for it, and are supported by their employer. There are also plenty of training courses for those wanting to become a member of the PR profession, which an employer may pay for as part of a training package if you are really sure this is the direction in which you want your career to progress.

In-house PR is totally focused on one organization and associated market sectors – some find this focus refreshing, allowing them to really explore a wide range of opportunities, and to integrate their work with other marketing and sales functions. However, over time this can also feel limiting, unless the organization grows or changes, and if PR is linked to a strong annual cycle, then it can also become a little repetitive.

Career progression in-house can also be limited. The PRO usually fulfils a specific, discrete role, and although responsibilities will grow as the company grows, the job itself may not change dramatically or lead to another position. Some PROs are perfectly happy with this, especially those who don't want any more responsibility, but for those with real ambition, this can be a drawback. In larger companies, PROs can reach director level, but in many organizations PROs report to the Marketing Director, whilst rarely moving up to the Board. As a result, in-house PROs usually further their careers by moving from company to company, perhaps to gain the responsibilities of managing a larger team, or to work in a different industry sector or environment. In-house PROs often move into agencies in order to broaden their experience and perhaps gain the seniority denied by the structure of their current employer. In the same way, consultants often move in-house, perhaps because they have developed specific expertise which they now want to exploit or swap the variety of agency life for the concentrated effort of the in-house post.

It's also important to remember that PR career paths often switch from in-house to consultancy and back again, so making that initial choice doesn't mean that you've set your future in stone.

GAINING EXPERIENCE

As in so many very popular professions, proven experience can really help you get that all-important first job. As we've already noted, competition for PR vacancies (especially entry level posts in larger agencies) can be daunting, and having some real PR knowledge is clearly a plus, even more so if you're up for the job against PR degree graduates, who may already have had work experience as part of their degree course.

It's the classic catch 22 – you can't get a job without experience, but without a job you can't experience. How can you break the cycle?:

Work as a PR intern or 'volunteer'
Some larger agencies run internship or work experience programmes, giving college level students the chance to work (usually for no or very little pay) within the agency for a limited period. Internships

aim to give students experience – you won't be given any real responsibility but you will be allowed to see exactly how the agency operates. Such schemes are only offered by the largest agencies, usually based in the larger cities, and competition for places is intense. However, you can always approach PR organizations or businesses more local to you, and see if they'll take you on perhaps as unpaid help over the summer months, making it clear that you are keen to gain PR experience of any kind. Clearly, financially, this option needs to be considered carefully.

Exploit experience gained in another career path

Many PROs enter the industry from another profession or discipline. As we've already noted, many are former journalists, exploiting their proven writing skills and knowledge of the media. They tend to work on media liaison campaigns, as they often lack (initially at least) the wider skill set required to run a broader campaign. But remember that broad experience is also more valuable than narrow – in an agency in particular you might have to work with clients from a wide range of industry sectors, and general knowledge can be invaluable in such circumstances.

Marketing professionals often move into PR as in most firms PR comes within the marketing remit and so marketing staff often find that PR (at some level) comes within their brief. In fact, the divide between marketing and PR is often fairly blurred as marketeers often find themselves involved in activities which equal those used in a PR campaign – such as sponsorship programmes, events, exhibitions and copywriting. If you've shown an aptitude for this type of activity then you can already demonstrate evidence of the core skills required, standing you in good stead when you start to look for more specific PR roles.

PROs also come from completely 'opposite' professions. For example, some scientists welcome the opportunity to communicate and may develop a skill in writing general articles or speaking to the lay public about what they do and why it's so important. A scientist who can write and who can talk cogently to journalists, who can clearly explain a complex issue or development could become a great PRO, especially in a scientific or technical agency, or in a company operating within those fields.

Developing skills as a PR 'amateur'
If you are interested in PR and the way it works, then you may well have already tried your hand at some of the activities described in this book – not within your work but in your private life. Have you ever had to publicize an event (for example a school fete or fundraiser), and found yourself ringing journalists and arranging photographers? Do you write and edit a newsletter? Have you started or helped to run a campaign on a local, national or international issue? Did you find yourself thinking of all possible ways to generate publicity? PR experience of all sorts is important – it shows you are really interested in the profession, and already have some of the skills required, no matter how basic the level. Many PR firms appoint trainees because of their potential to deliver, rather than their immediate ability, so don't dismiss your 'amateur' PR – it could be just as valuable as any other experience.

TEST YOURSELF

What is the ideal PR team profile for the following organizations?:

▶ A small to medium sized organization planning a limited campaign comprising mainly 'high-level', highly targeted activities.

▶ A large company planning an international consumer campaign, starting with a major product launch.

▶ A local information service running a number of small-scale activities targeted at a variety of audiences, needing to repeat the same messages in a number of different ways.

11

Evaluating success

In this chapter you will learn:
- **how to set measurable aims and objectives**
- **evaluation techniques**

A common criticism of Public Relations is that it is difficult to evaluate effectively, and it's easy to see why. PR is often implemented in order to achieve goals such as 'raising awareness', or 'enhancing relations with key groups'. Although these are valid aims, they are often couched in such nebulous terms that it is difficult to imagine how to start to measure such concepts as awareness. But nevertheless, effective evaluation is vital – otherwise, how can you be sure that your programme is achieving its overall objectives, and that your budget is being wisely spent?

Setting measurable aims and objectives

In setting parameters for your evaluation process, it's important to revisit the aims and objectives of your PR programme – and to recap, we defined aims as being your overarching goals, and objectives as the practical means by which you will achieve these goals. It is the objectives which are translated into tangible PR activities.

If you want to evaluate something, then you need to be able to assess it in the context of a *measurable* aim or objective. If you can't measure it, in some form or other (and we'll look at how to define this term in more detail shortly), then how can you tell if you've achieved it? It's also crucial that these aims and objectives are realistic – both in terms of the nature of your organization, and the level of success you can realistically hope to achieve, at least within the timeframe of your evaluation period. You may want to appear on the front page of the *Financial Times*, for example, but in reality, is it ever going to happen? Perhaps if your organization suddenly becomes incredibly newsworthy (and this may be for negative as well as positive reasons) then it may occur, but if not then don't expect PR to achieve miracles. But by setting more attainable goals – say, 'to issue regular, relevant material to key financial media' – you can take the first step towards your ultimate aim, probably gaining some worthwhile results along the way.

Let's look at some examples, and identify the ways in which an aim can be evaluated with some degree of rigour – and then we'll look more closely at practical evaluation activities to see how they work. For the purposes of this exercise we have been deliberately simplistic – each of the aims listed below could well be translated into a broader range of objectives, but at least they give some idea of how to begin the process:

Aim	Objective	Evaluation
To become known by consumers as a leading supplier of Product X.	To gain increased coverage within identified consumer media.	Monitor and evaluate press coverage within identified consumer media.
To raise the profile of our organization among financial directors of blue chip companies.	To produce a discursive newsletter, addressing issues of interest and relevance.	Use a high-quality mailing list to ensure newsletter is received by right people; analyse feedback mechanisms incorporated into newsletter.

Aim	Objective	Evaluation
To make local business advisers aware of service X, and of the benefits it could offer their clients.	Hold a launch event designed specifically to attract that audience, backed by a targeted media and promotional campaign.	Use a targeted mailing list to ensure the information is received by all members of target group; analyse profile of guests attending event; analyse media coverage.

However, before you begin to evaluate, it's also important to keep in mind the context within which your PR campaign has been operating, as this also has an impact upon the end result. For example, you may consider the budget for your PR campaign to be very generous, but how does it compare to your advertising spend, or your exhibition budget? If you are expecting to identify a direct contribution to the bottom line, then make sure it's along the same percentages as your budget division. Also make sure that any analysis takes notice of other marketing activities taking place at the same time. If you are concentrating solely on PR, then it's easier to assess its impact – if you are also running major online, direct mail and advertising campaigns, then your target groups will be exposed to information from a variety of sources, and you may need to weight your final evaluation accordingly, while also factoring in sales, profits or other business metrics which may not become apparent for some time.

Insight

To evaluate PR effectively, link each activity to realistic, measureable and achievable goals. Don't be too ambitious at the outset – for example, the goal for an ezine may simply be to ensure regular contact with a key target audience, rather than generating an immediate increase in sales.

Evaluation techniques

Now let's look at some different types of evaluation techniques, so that you can identify the most appropriate to your own strategy.

AWARENESS SURVEY

If 'raising general awareness' is one of your central aims, and you really want to get an accurate assessment of how well your programme has performed, then a two-stage awareness survey is the only real way of achieving this – but unfortunately probably the most expensive. In brief, you must survey your target audiences prior to the launch of your PR campaign, or before a major activity such as a sponsorship or new product launch, and establish levels of awareness – for example, the level of familiarity with your name or brand, a rating against competitor products or organizations, and an awareness of other related issues if pertinent. The PR campaign is then launched, runs for a predetermined period, and the survey is then repeated. A comparison of results will show if your PR strategy has resulted in a significant increase in awareness amongst your target audience. An awareness survey differs from a communications audit (see page 159) primarily in its aims – you want to establish levels of awareness, not the means by which it was generated.

This is an expensive exercise, and so only really relevant if your proposed PR spend is significant, and your target audience large enough to survey effectively – major brands, household names, large corporations use this technique because they need to be highly sensitive to changes in the perceptions of their target audiences, and need evidence to prove the success (or otherwise) of highly expensive campaigns. But if you are a small or medium organization, and if your brand or product range is well defined, then such an exercise may be too much. Alternatively, you could use focus groups for more in-depth analysis of awareness, or include related questions on other market research activities. New customers are often asked where they first heard about an organization, and if 'it has a local reputation for ….' (you can fill in the blank, or even give some options) is added to the list of responses then this could generate some relevant feedback.

EVALUATING MEDIA LIAISON CAMPAIGNS

As media liaison is often such an important element within a campaign, it's important that it is evaluated as thoroughly as possible, and there are a number of distinct activities which you could undertake, listed below. (Note: for the purposes of this section, we're referring to broadcast, print and online media – social media is detailed later.):

Monitoring media coverage

One of the best and most obvious ways of assessing the success of your media liaison programme (and, by implication, the relevance of the information that you are sending to the media), is to monitor, record and analyse all media coverage you gain. If your programme is operating on a small scale, and your media list is very limited, then you may be able to handle this in-house – you know who is receiving your press releases, so simply read, watch or listen to those media and record the instances when your name appears. (Note: If national newspapers are included in your press list, you must make sure you have the right to reproduce and circulate press cuttings within your organization and beyond. If you are in the UK, for example, then make sure you register with the Newspaper Licensing Agency (NLA) – this was established in 1996 to enable organizations to lawfully copy newspaper press cuttings for internal management purposes. Full details of how to register and obtain a licence, plus lists of the publications which come under this regulation, can be found at the NLA's website. If you are monitoring coverage from elsewhere in the world, then check to see what local rules and laws apply.)

It doesn't take long, however, for even a modest media campaign to start to generate results, and for your organization to receive wider coverage than originally expected, and so if you want to get a better picture of who is covering you in the media then it's time to get professional help from a media monitoring agency. A quick online search will soon provide links to a number of such agencies – as you'll discover, they provide a wide range of national and international services, covering print, broadcast and online media, and can advise on distribution, evaluation and a host of other issues beside. If you only had trade coverage in mind, don't be put off by the apparent size of some of these agencies, and the nature of their client list. They can just as easily service a more modest account, and can provide estimates on request. Placed against the cost of buying, reading, watching and monitoring all that media yourself, an agency may soon seem quite reasonable.

You can also ask agencies to monitor other key words or trends, if you want to gain a better idea of the context in which a campaign will be launched, which is often important if you are championing a cause, trying to create real market differentiation, or know you may need to educate an audience as well as inform them.

Assessing the value of media coverage

Once you've started to log your coverage, then you need to evaluate its effectiveness. The traditional, numerical count of column centimeters or broadcast seconds – although often gratifying – is not enough. You need to look more closely at the type of coverage you've received, and the benefits you've gained from it. Once again, media monitoring agencies can provide an ongoing, indepth analysis of coverage as it is received, but this is more useful if you generate regular, widespread coverage, often independent of your specific PR work, or you want continuous assessment because you may need to change tactics (think political campaigns). However, if you simply want to evaluate a relatively modest media campaign, then consider the following criteria when looking at the coverage you've gained:

▶ **Vehicle:** *Was the coverage gained in the right places? In your key target media or those you were not so bothered about?*
▶ **Placement:** *Where did your information appear? For example, if it was featured in a key trade magazine, was it in the most appropriate section? If it was in the local newspaper, was nicely up front or buried at the back? Likewise, did your news make the headlines on the radio or TV programme which featured it, or was it used for light relief – or worse, were you filmed or recorded and then not featured at all?*
▶ **Presentation:** *Was a photo used (and did you have to pay for it?); what was the headline; was the whole press release used or just the first paragraph (or less)?*
▶ **Quality:** *Is the copy accurate? If you are mentioned within a broader news story or other analytical feature, is your*

*organization given positive, neutral or negative coverage?
Were you quoted verbatim, edited or – worse – misquoted?*

▶ **Positive or negative?:** *If coverage was not simply factual, was it positive or negative? If negative, why?*

▶ **Competition:** *Did anything steal the limelight just when you were hoping to make a major splash (is it worth, in fact, reissuing the news again if it was smothered by a story which broke unexpectedly)? Did similar news from rival organizations gain better exposure than your own? Can you tell why?*

▶ **Feedback:** *Have you been able to directly attribute any response to the coverage you received, such as spikes in website visits immediately after the coverage was gained, or calls from reps or suppliers? And don't forget the quality of the feedback – you may be getting a lot of enquiries but are they from your key target groups? And if not, why not?*

▶ **Unsolicited coverage:** *How much coverage was gained without your direct involvement? Perhaps you were mentioned in the context of another article or your MD was quoted in a news report. Is this increasing or not? Is the coverage received in this way positive or negative? How many of the unsolicited calls that you've received from journalists have turned into valuable coverage?*

You also need to identify, in due course, the media which did not feature your news, by logging coverage against your original distribution list. Don't start this review too quickly – if your news was not time critical (a contract announcement for example, or a case history) then a publication may well hold it back until the next edition. You may find that some press releases are still generating coverage months after you originally dispatched them. If you find that your news is rarely being covered, then review your press release style and your distribution list – perhaps your news simply isn't relevant for the media you've identified. Perhaps you're being too ambitious. Perhaps you're not supplying the type of information the magazine or programme wants to receive. You'll probably find that the 'B' list media are those which rarely cover your news, so clean your list, reducing it to those media you know are showing a sustained interest, and reserving the other titles and programmes for those occasions when you have something more relevant to say.

To follow on from this last point, in Chapter 3 we mentioned that you should never phone a journalist to ask why a press release wasn't used, except in exceptional circumstances. If your material is consistently ignored, however, this could constitute the exception, and so it may be worth ringing someone on the editorial team to gently enquire why this is happening so frequently. You may discover that the publication in question has very strict rules concerning press submissions about which you were unaware – and this can happen if you don't review your media list regularly. Some publications only want press releases of 100 words, for example, or you may have been sending your material to the wrong email address. This type of neutral call, not linked to any specific press release or campaign, may also lead onto a longer conversation about other material which may be relevant.

So, just when you thought that gaining media coverage was enough of an achievement in itself, you now realize how much more you have to think about! As you can imagine, for major multinational organizations, the monitoring and analysis of media coverage becomes an all-important routine which goes on around the clock. But in reality, the results of a modest media liaison campaign will be relatively easy to assess – you'll know the value of the magazines or programmes in which you were featured, and already have a fair idea of the sections in which your releases are most likely to gain coverage. But nevertheless, it's worth having these assessment criteria in the back of your mind as you look over the coverage you've received. You need to be sure that the type of coverage you are generating reflects the quality of the information you are putting out, and if not why not?

Insight

If media monitoring is an important evaluation tool, and your target media list is wide, consider exploring the services of a specialist agency able to monitor media coverage and evaluate success. Incorporate feedback mechanisms into other PR activities to provide additional feedback information.

Evaluating social media tools

As mentioned in Chapter 3, if social media is a key part of your PR strategy, then hiring a social media specialist may be wise, not only to assist with the technical skills required, but also to plan the most effective campaign, and then to evaluate the results realistically. And 'realistically' is the key word here – you may theoretically be reaching thousands, even millions, of people as your messages multiply virally around the globe, but what contribution has that made to your PR aims, and what percentage of these millions is made up of your target audiences? Fans and followers may give you an easy metric for 'success', but once again, the quality of that audience is what's important, and how that quality equates to your aims – has it directly influenced sales enquiries, for example, or increased tangible support for a specific cause, perhaps expressed through donations?

In addition, the focus of social media on comment and personality may have unexpected results which you may have to monitor. Have you actually found it hard work to provide opinions on a regular basis, and is anyone listening? This will be easier to determine for an issue-led campaign, but not perhaps if you are making a widget for trade markets. Likewise, is a focus on personality reaping any rewards? Again, this could work well for a business where personal contact is important, but could appear unnecessary if your staff rarely interact with end-users.

However, if your audience includes a younger demographic, then simply demonstrating that your company is comfortable with social media tools may be enough to satisfy your basic evaluation (back to taking small steps, again), as by doing so you have demonstrated your awareness of what's important to this target group, and are communicating your messages in the way this group wants to hear them. As tools and audiences develop, you can then move on to a more detailed analysis of the benefits this may be bringing your organization. Sooner or later you'll need to see more tangible evidence that your spend in this area – in time and in money – has been worth it, and worth more than similar effort expended in more 'traditional' activities, which is where specialist help could prove invaluable.

Using direct feedback mechanisms

If possible, include a 'feedback mechanism' within every PR activity – use your judgement to decide how overt you want this to be, depending upon the nature of the vehicle or activity you are implementing. The results will provide you with the raw data essential to a full understanding of the success or otherwise of the exercise you undertook. For example, here are some feedback mechanisms relating to specific activities:

Material issued to the media

Always make sure that a web address is included at the bottom of every item released to the media – it won't always be published, but if it is, you can measure any related spikes in visitors to your website around the time the story appeared. Record any feedback which can be attributed directly to specific coverage – visitors to specific product pages, for example, direct calls referencing the coverage, competition entries, and don't forget to note any contact you've had with journalists.

Events

A delegate questionnaire can be used to generate instant feedback from almost any type of event. It's best not to make such forms too long or difficult – if your delegates don't hand them back at the end of the event then it's unlikely they will remember to do so later – and use multiple choice questions as much as possible. Incentives, such as entry into a prize draw, can also encourage an increased return, but only use this device if you feel it fits in with the tone of the occasion. As well as including such questionnaires in delegate packs, you can also hand them out to guests as they leave, or post or email them on afterwards.

Newsletters, ezines, literature and websites
It seems obvious, but don't forget to put contact details on all materials, produced as part of your PR campaign, possibly using dedicated email addresses if you want to measure impact with even greater accuracy. Newsletters provide an ideal opportunity to include more specific email contacts – sales directors, representatives etc., who may be of interest to your target audiences, and help you judge the interest in each specific story. As we discussed in Chapter 4, the infrequent inclusion of a questionnaire can also be used to gain more detailed information. A direct incentive (a bribe in other words) to return the questionnaire will certainly up your return rate, and may be considered a worthwhile investment if you really want to find out the views of your readership.

Make sure your website gets plenty of mentions as well – directing as much traffic as possible onto a well-designed website can deliver significant added value, and can once again help provide a valuable filter.

Your IT team or web manager will also be able to analyse the response to your ezine, looking at who opened what features – sometimes you can even see how much of an article was read before the reader clicked away. You want to know how much PR has contributed in general to an increase in web traffic, and if that has been translated into more tangible actions. The quality of contact is important – it's not enough just to know that more people have visited your site, but are they of the right quality, or of direct relevance, and are they taking it further? The response gained from information request forms or email queries should provide some answers.

Sponsorships
See Chapter 5 for more on the specific evaluation of Sponsorship activities.

Indirect feedback

As your PR campaign progresses, you should also begin to get a 'feel' for how well things are going simply as a result of the daily conversations you have with your target audiences. Start to make a note of any interesting comments such as 'we saw you in the paper the other day', and try to evaluate how familiar your name has become (and social media may help you in this, if you can evaluate it effectively). It may seem all rather nebulous, but gut feeling does play a role in the whole process and so shouldn't be ignored. In particular, note any occasion when a client or contact makes specific reference to recent coverage. It's also not unusual for first time customers to be asked how they heard about a company (whether in person, or by an online or other form of questionnaire). Often respondents cannot pin down a specific reason but if you add 'local reputation' to the list of options then you may find out how important a role reputation plays.

Canvass other sections within your organization to see if they are handling more enquiries, or have received more positive feedback from existing customers, or from suppliers or other contacts. It can all help you gather together evidence to indicate whether or not your PR plan is on the right track.

Insight

A PR campaign can generate significant interest, so make sure staff are prepared for any success as this is another element of the evaluation process. You don't want to end up with a damaged reputation because you couldn't deal with the interest you set out to encourage.

Dealing with success

It's one thing to run a successful PR campaign and to generate lots of leads, but you then have to capitalize upon this interest.

If your sales and marketing teams are unable to convert quality leads into promising sales contacts then all your hard work will be undone, and it's important to remember this when analysing the effectiveness of the strategy as a whole, especially its contribution to bottom line. It's also important to back fine words with concrete actions. As we noted in Chapter 7, one of the most common grievances noted by staff when it comes to considering corporate communications is that a company will say one thing whilst doing the opposite. Once you have started to establish a clearer image in the public eye, it's important that you strive to live up to that image or else run the risk of undermining all the good that your programme has achieved on your behalf.

STAFF RESPONSE

We've already noted the importance of keeping your staff, your sales team, distributors or representatives informed of your PR programme. They need to know – ahead of time – if a press release is about to be issued, so that they can be prepared for increase in interest, and can talk knowledgeably about any press coverage that has been received. This is particularly important if you expect to generate a lot of publicity at once – a product launch for example, or the announcement of a new service or technology. We've all read about companies who have been unable to keep up with the demand that their promotional activities have generated and as a result, ironically, generating much negative PR. Of course, you need to judge exactly which staff should know what, but whatever you decide to tell them, anything is better than nothing.

Evaluation – how often?

How often should you evaluate your PR campaign? Although this does depend greatly upon the mix of activities you've chosen to implement, evaluation should be carried out regularly, to ensure that the programme remains on track, and also – over the longer term – in order to identify any positive trends that could be exploited, or negative trends that should be investigated. If you have launched a very specific, time critical campaign (leading up to a specific event) then you'll probably want to evaluate as you go along, tailoring activities if necessary, and then saving a fuller debriefing until after the dust has settled.

For more longer term, sustained PR campaigns, evaluation should be a stock item on the agenda of your regular PR meeting: look at issues such as media coverage, journalist contact and review any feedback from specific events. Depending upon the extent of your programme, also aim to undertake a more in-depth review either six-monthly or annually, when you can generate a comprehensive list of what has been achieved, and can analyse the contribution of each element within the programme. At this stage you can also try to identify areas of concern, areas of success and directions in which to move forward. Evaluation is a crucial element of the next stage of your PR programme – planning next year's strategy – so good luck!

TEST YOURSELF

Which evaluation mechanisms would you employ to assess:

▶ *A Christmas party for business contacts?*

▶ *A seminar?*

▶ *A syndicated competition?*

▶ *A trade press release?*

PR Matrix

Time to complete the Matrix. You'll now need to add a final column, Evaluation, and for each activity that you've identified, list precisely the terms by which you'll evaluate its success.

Now all you need to do is put the whole programme into action!

Taking it further

Some useful contacts

The Chartered Institute of Public Relations (IPR)
www.cipr.co.uk

Public Relations Consultants Association (PRCA)
www.prca.org.uk

The Public Relations Society of America (PRSA)
www.prsa.org

PR Week (UK)
www.prweek.com/uk/home

PR Week (US)
www.prweekus.com

Newspaper Licensing Agency (NLA)
www.nla.co.uk

Index